D0160991

From Anxiety to Meltdown

by the same author

Managing Meltdowns
Using the S.C.A.R.E.D. Calming Technique with
Children and Adults with Autism
Deborah Lipsky and Will Richards
ISBN 978 1 84310 908 2

of related interest

No Fighting, No Biting, No Screaming
How to Make Behaving Positively Possible for People
with Autism and Other Developmental Disabilities
Bo Hejlskov Elvén
ISBN 978 1 84905 126 2

Managing Family Meltdown
The Low Arousal Approach and Autism
Linda Woodcock and Andrea Page
Foreword by Andrew McDonnell
ISBN 978 1 84905 009 8

People with Autism Behaving Badly
Helping People with ASD Move On from
Behavioral and Emotional Challenges
John Clements
ISBN 978 1 84310 765 1

From Anxiety to Meltdown

How Individuals on the Autism
Spectrum Deal with Anxiety, Experience
Meltdowns, Manifest Tantrums, and
How You Can Intervene Effectively

DEBORAH LIPSKY

Jessica Kingsley *Publishers*
London and Philadelphia

First published in 2011
by Jessica Kingsley Publishers
116 Pentonville Road
London N1 9JB, UK
and
400 Market Street, Suite 400
Philadelphia, PA 19106, USA

www.jkp.com

Copyright © Deborah Lipsky 2011

All rights reserved. No part of this publication may be reproduced in any material
form (including photocopying or storing it in any medium by electronic means and
whether or not transiently or incidentally to some other use of this publication)
without the written permission of the copyright owner except in accordance with the
provisions of the Copyright, Designs and Patents Act 1988 or under the terms of a
licence issued by the Copyright Licensing Agency Ltd, Saffron House, 6–10 Kirby
Street, London EC1N 8TS. Applications for the copyright owner's written permission
to reproduce any part of this publication should be addressed to the publisher.

Warning: The doing of an unauthorised act in relation to a copyright work
may result in both a civil claim for damages and criminal prosecution.

Library of Congress Cataloging in Publication Data
Lipsky, Deborah.
  From anxiety to meltdown-- : how individuals on the autism spectrum deal
with anxiety, experience meltdowns, manifest tantrums, and how you can
intervene effectively / Deborah Lipsky.
    p. cm.
  ISBN 978-1-84905-843-8 (alk. paper)
  1. Autism spectrum disorders. 2. Anxiety. 3. Temper tantrums. 4. Crisis
intervention (Mental health services) I. Title.
  RC553.A88L567 2011
  616.85'882--dc22
                                   2010047566

British Library Cataloguing in Publication Data
A CIP catalogue record for this book is available from the British Library

ISBN 978 1 84905 843 8

Printed and bound in the United States

Contents

8. Communication Triggers that Cause Meltdowns 191

9. Meltdown Interventions 215

Introduction

Shortly after my diagnosis of high functioning autism in 2005 I created a training program for the Autism Society of Maine for emergency room staff at hospitals to deal with avoiding meltdowns in individuals on the spectrum. In 2008, with the help of my co-author, we took this training program, expounded on it, and formatted it into a manual to be used to de-escalate a meltdown in progress. In 2009 it was published by Jessica Kingsley Publishers under the title *Managing Meltdowns: Using the S.C.A.R.E.D. Calming Technique with Children and Adults with Autism.* This "book" was designed to be used as a practical manual during a meltdown to de-escalate the situation. In an easy and quick to read format it gives strategies on how to de-escalate rising meltdowns complete with dos and don'ts. Written in an understandable language for the average person I formatted this book with first responders in mind, such as policemen, ambulance attendants, teachers and their aides, baby sitters, and basically any caregiver witnessing an escalation phase in progress. It is helpful for non verbal and verbal individuals on the autism spectrum regardless of their severity. This second book is something of a "pre-quell" to the meltdown book in the sense that it will 'cover in depth the role anxiety plays in meltdowns, catastrophic reactions, and behaviors of all sorts. It picks up where the other book left off, explaining why we behave the way we do and how you as the reader can better understand what motivates that anxiety.

Since I began doing seminars I have always devoted the afternoon session to meltdowns, tantrums, behaviors, how to recognize their triggers, onset, and deal effectively with them. At every seminar since then attendees have strongly urged me to write a book on this topic, which they found most helpful, mainly because I have the ability to describe what is going on inside our heads as we begin to escalate. This book will offer you a rare glimpse into the thought process of an individual with autism from a true expert... one who is autistic herself. When I do behavioral consults I act as an "interpreter." I observe the individual in the environment causing the explosive behavior. Being autistic myself I "pick up" on unrecognized environmental triggers. I listen intently to the verbal interactions from those directly working with the individual. If the instructions come across as vague or confusing to me they will also be to the child. I have many similar difficulties regarding the environment I am exposed to and am therefore much more in tune with stressors that may go unrecognized by the non autistic person. While all people with autism are very different we all share many of the same traits that unite those of us on the autism spectrum.

Despite my master's degree in education and counseling I am unable to live independently. I have poor executive functioning skills revolving around daily life skills as well as many safety issues. For instance, I have such a high tolerance to pain that would immobilize another individual that I am not aware of its severity. At times in the past I have had life threatening injuries and/or illnesses, but if it hadn't been for my family or friends literally taking me by the hand and to the hospital I would not be here writing this book. We will look at how pain thresholds play a significant and dangerous role in catastrophic reactions and why self injurious behavior seems to cause no immediate discomfort to the individual engaging in head banging or self biting.

Prior to my diagnosis I had a history of sudden explosive behavior when things didn't go according to plan, with what to the casual observer seemed exaggerated reactions over trivial matters. These "reactions" were in fact unrecognized meltdowns. I was constantly told to "pull myself together," or "grow up and stop tantruming." I remember feeling horribly frustrated at these comments because as I began to spiral downward it become impossible for me to self regulate and control my behaviors. It was as if I was being held hostage by my own mind; the more I tried to calm myself down once I escalated, the more my brain began shutting down.

Newly diagnosed, I felt somewhat vindicated by the fact that my autism was responsible for these "outbursts." I read all the books I could find on the subject of meltdowns, which weren't that many. I was deeply disappointed. The books I read interchanged meltdown with tantrums and recommended behavioral and sometimes punitive responses with the misguided notion that it was a willful manipulative behavior. Other books claimed that autistic individuals simply must learn to adapt to all environments. No one was explaining accurately what was driving our unusually strong reactions. No one was recommending that caregivers should understand we had limits and despite interventions such as desensitization we could not overcome certain things. The current philosophy that autism is a terrible disease and the push to get children with autism "normalized" is overshadowing the fact that we do not have a disease, we are just different, and that we cannot be "normal" in the sense that mainstream society expects. Sensory issues, communication, language barriers, all create at times insurmountable obstacles due to our neurological processing differences.

In this book we will examine how our anxiety is inherent to autism and is part of our personality as opposed to something that should be automatically medicated away or desensitized. Triggers that cause anxiety levels to rise beyond our control will be identified. Many forms of behaviors such as crying, screaming, bolting, aggression, or complete disengaging from those around us may be a tantrum or may be an instinctual response to a meltdown. This book will give you the keys to differentiating between a meltdown and tantrum and more importantly how to deal with them effectively. If you use meltdown strategies for tantrums you may be rewarding bad behavior, yet tantrum or Applied Behavior Analysis (ABA) punitive measures for meltdowns will create even more distress and be of no help. Sometimes tantrums can become established due to inappropriate strategies from well meaning caregivers trying to avoid meltdowns. This book will discuss some very common mistakes made in handling behaviors and better ways of dealing with them. Meltdowns and ways to avoid them will be covered in depth. We will also look at many issues that create difficulties such as a single parent working multiple jobs with a child on the spectrum and other non autistic siblings, individuals with autism living in group homes where constant staff turnover creates behaviors, going to the dentist or doctor, family divorce, moving, etc. While there will be no immediate solution for some of these issues I will offer you a better understanding of our needs in those environments.

This is a book that will benefit any parent, caregiver, or professional greatly by explaining why we react so strongly to seemingly minor changes and it offers vital effective strategies for dealing with these issues. For those individuals on the spectrum this book will give you the needed affirmation that we aren't "doing it for attention," or being bad willfully. Understanding and recognizing your own personal triggers will be a major benefit in developing a plan to avoid the unabated anxiety levels that lead to meltdowns. To me autism isn't a disorder but rather a cultural difference, and we should learn to cohabit in a symbiotic relationship as opposed to the current trend of forcing individuals with autism to conform to a society that is inherently foreign. Both sides need to find common ground and the more we understand each other's differences and how that affects our thought processes the easier it will become to bridge the seemingly large gap between the autistic and non autistic population.

Chapter 1

Seeing the World Through Our Eyes

To fully comprehend why we have such strong negative reactions to seemingly minor daily disruptions one must understand how the autistic population perceives the world. We will look at the core "issues" of autism from the perspective of someone who lives it daily. Actually I don't like using the term "core issues" because it seems to have a negative overtone. Let's instead view them as "core character traits." It is paramount that you the reader should not misunderstand the word "autism" to truly appreciate the insights this book will offer. On the television and in the media autism mostly carries a negative connotation. It is a "disease," "disorder," "lifelong burden," and, my favorite, an "epidemic." Many people have a stereotypical view of an autistic individual as a non verbal child who rocks incessantly, huddles in a corner flapping their hands, and seems to wail when asked to do something. Society has not fully accepted the higher functioning person with autism and Asperger's as an individual who despite looking physically "normal" does have limitations and special needs. I find this especially true in the school system. So many parents have lamented to me that, despite a diagnosis of autism, their child is not seen as "autistic" because they are doing well academically and therefore isn't offered the reasonable accommodations necessary to provide a safe learning environment for them. When I am called in for consultations due to "behavioral issues" by the school, most often these behaviors are the direct result of a lack of understanding of the child's particular needs as well as an incorrect understanding of what autism truly is.

News reports describe the insurmountable obstacles parents face, and the need to find a cure along with stopping the spread of autism. Every now and then a news story breaks about some incredible feat of an autistic individual and it seems more of an aberration to the world than a true measure of the gifts and capabilities all individuals on the spectrum have. There is an almost obsessive drive to purge autistic traits out of these children so that they can act "normal" and successfully integrate with society. For a culture that embraces diversity, yet singles out autism as something that must be eradicated from the face of the world, this is counterproductive. Autism is more of a cultural difference than a disorder. The autistic population is rising dramatically. Perhaps one day we will outnumber the non autistic population.

I like to tell my audience that people with autism are like tigers. A tiger's natural environment where they are content doing what comes naturally and instinctively to them is the jungle. You can put us in the circus and train us to jump through hoops—for that is what is expected of tigers so that they fit in an environment not their own. Still a tiger is a tiger and has natural instincts that at best may be subdued or dormant for a while but can break forth at any time. People shouldn't be shocked when a wild animal such as a tiger suddenly and without warning snaps and attacks its trainer. Children on the spectrum are expected through much intervention to adapt themselves into a foreign world that goes against their natural "nature." It is no surprise that tantrums, meltdowns, and bad behaviors "break forth" without any reason apparent to the non autistic bystander. Understanding our thought processing differences will help you, the reader, better anticipate the outside influences that may create an extreme response despite the best behavioral plan or interventions.

Is autism part of an evolutionary process?

Why is autism on the rise? Every species must adapt in order to ensure its survival. What if nature is trying a new experiment by creating a blend of autistic and non autistic traits to create a new race of beings to ensure mankind's survival? Could you imagine a world where people said what they meant and meant what they said? Where honesty and truth abound? Our world is standing on the brink of extinction from terrorists, radical extremists, and an indifference to the abuse of our planet's natural resources. In generations yet to be born a blend of autistic and non autistic character traits in each human being may just ensure our continuity as a species. It is human emotion that may lead humanity to extinction. If you do not believe this then read about American life in the 1950s and the Cold War with Communism. I still remember air raid drills in 1966 for predicted atomic bomb attacks by the "Reds" (Soviet Union). Society became so paranoid about mass extinction it influenced every fiber of its being. People began building personal bomb shelters, magazine advertising catered to nuclear preparedness, and children were taught and drilled in the school system on how to survive a nuclear holocaust. Both the Soviet Union and the United States began building up its arsenal of weapons of mass destruction out of sheer fear the other side would attack. I collect items from Cold War America, including booklets, advertisements, and trinkets to increase the odds of surviving such an attack. Logic and reason took a backseat to raw emotional fear. No wonder the children of that era who became teenagers in the 1960s rebeled against authority with their famous mantra, "Make love and not war."

I collect these items as it is my way of understanding how being non autistic and slave to emotions can be a greater disability at times than having autism. It is comical to behold items that would not help the individual in any way during an atomic war, despite their claims, but people's emotions clouded logic and they bought these items to ease their anxiety. The McCarthy hearings (or witch hunt) during that time accused a lot of innocent people, including celebrities, of being Communist sympathizers, based not on hard evidence but on hearsay. Many people's careers were permanently destroyed as a result. This would never have happened in a dominantly autistic society.

What would our world look like if everyone kept to their scripts, for instance, airlines always leaving on time or being honest and announcing delays in a prompt manner? My speaking takes me all over the country so I fly a lot. It is so frustrating to be waiting at the gate for your departure, noting the departure time has passed, but the monitor board still displays the original and now incorrect departure time. You ask the airline representative behind the gate counter what the new departure time will be and generally they respond by saying they don't know. You ask for some timeframe for the delay yet receive a well rehearsed phrase that is cold and impartial. Someone has to know, don't they?

Wouldn't it make more sense during the pre-flight safety briefing by the airline attendant if she no longer stated that in case of water landing (let's be brutally honest and say what you really mean… crash) your seat cushion doubles as a flotation device, and instead gives clear concise instructions on how to use the parachute and open the windows which act as emergency exits located in each row? A society predominantly autistic would familiarize themselves with emergency escape procedures well in advance of the flight. If you were an unlucky passenger not familiar with this critical knowledge your fellow autistic passenger would be prepared to give you a discourse on proper evacuation procedures. To minimize the casualty rate in such catastrophic events an autistic society would engineer planes that complement our need to script out every scenario including disasters. Basic logic will tell you that four emergency exits for a plane that holds 230-plus people, with only a 90-second window to escape, is eerily reminiscent of the lack of enough lifeboats to hold every passenger on the Titanic. To up the survival statistics autistically engineered planes would give every passenger an equal chance of beating those odds by adding in structural features which take into account the fact that accidents may happen (due to our need to script for just about every contingency). I constantly question the non autistic rationale of so few exits for so many airplane passengers but I keep getting the answer, "You can't worry about the unknown, so just don't think about it." When I ask fellow passengers what they would do in the event of an impending crash, overwhelmingly the response I get is, "Well I would just put my head between my legs and kiss my behind goodbye."

I challenge you to contemplate the real disability here. What is worse? The emotional distress of the mere thought of a disaster that makes one unable to plan for the unexpected so that they resign themselves to dying in a fiery ball of flames, or the individual who analyzes planes crashes and comes up with viable options to increase their survival in such an event and isn't even selfish with this knowledge, using it as "small talk" to engage their fellow row mates? Trust me, right now if I engage others while waiting in airports with Doomsday crash scenario scripts I am seen as a lunatic, but if the plane were really going down and I stood up saying I knew how to improve our odds of surviving I bet I would be seen as a savior.

The importance of scripts

Our need for having everything to follow scripts (a pre-set pattern of events) for even the most mundane daily life skills such as getting dressed or brushing teeth seems mind boggling to an outsider. Routines and rituals govern our every activity. I will elaborate much more on this in Chapter 4, but for now let's note that in many instances our staunch refusal to break our pattern or routine collides with the non autistic mindset that "variety is the spice of life." My non autistic husband is forever trying to persuade me to try a new dish when we go out for dinner at the same Italian restaurant. As sure as the sun rises each morning I always order the same thing, noodles Alfredo. I marvel at how he truly enjoys reading each entrée selection and then creates difficulties for himself because according to him there are so many dishes he would love to try and he can't make up his mind. Annoyingly I have to script in ten extra minutes on these dining excursions just for his indecisiveness over menu selection. Apparently to the non autistic population trying something new just to "excite" the palate seems pleasurable due to the thrill of the anticipation of unknown and unexperienced flavors. He is quick to remind me that, "You don't know what you are missing."

I retort with an expression I have learned that goes, "If it isn't broken then don't fix it." To me bland is beautiful and, since I am happy with my dinner selection which is very pleasurable to my taste buds, there is no need to deviate from what works for me.

Heightened senses impact our ability to navigate social settings

Most individuals with autism are very content with this seemingly narrow approach of avoiding new experiences, particularly in a society where everything is so unpredictable and constantly changing, often without any logical basis behind the change. Many individuals with autism have heightened senses so it is very common for us to experience sensory integration overload or difficulties in areas overlooked by non autistic people. The tongue is a sensory organ divided into sections where certain taste buds pick up on salty, sweet, sour, bitter, etc. Something as simple as spaghetti sauce may feel as spicy as jalapeño peppers to an autistic person with sensory issues. Once while at a church picnic I was sitting with a family who had a child with Asperger's Syndrome. This child was doing very well running around with three other children chasing butterflies. Seeing as it was a warm day one of the other mothers offered these children a cold drink, which happened to be ice cold soda pop from the picnic cooler. The boy with Asperger's Syndrome, who was seven years old and very thirsty, impulsively took a big swallow of this beverage and almost immediately went into a full meltdown. No one around, including his mother, knew what triggered this catastrophic reaction as he normally enjoyed drinking soda pop. Initially they assumed he was upset because either he didn't get served first, or that the wrong cup was used, and on and on they micro-analyzed what minor detail may have prompted his wailing. The mother attempted to quiet him down by offering him a new cup and new can of soda, which only escalated the situation and intensified his self stimming.

I knew immediately just by his non verbal reactions that this was a sensory issue so I ran up to him with a small cool, not ice cold, juice box which I placed in front of his face. He immediately grabbed it and began drinking. Within a few minutes he was calmed down.

I explained to the mother all about heightened senses and how sometimes the most mundane of things that non autistic people take for granted may not be so to the autistic population. In this young boy's situation it was the temperature variation of the soda fizz that became a sensory nightmare to him. Although he drank soda before it had never been that cold and the bubbly sensation of the fizz became unbearable. As a result for the rest of the picnic that little boy became fearful of all foods out of his comfort range and refused to eat or drink anything else while there. Of course I am not advocating that we should stay locked up in our rooms for ever to avoid unpleasant experiences in life. I am merely pointing out that seemingly ordinarily sensory sensations can be unbearable to individuals with autism. Actually, sensory overload has been perfected into a cruel means of torture. Throughout history various empires and regimes perfected the means of non lethal torture by employing methods that led to such sensory overloads as to cause insanity in the prisoner who was subjected to it for prolonged periods. So when individuals on the spectrum are subjected to sensory overloads without any means of escape from the stimulation it is a similar form of non lethal torture employing sensory overload methods.

A parent forcing a child with autism to go into a department store during the Christmas holiday season, even if it is just for five minutes to "teach" them to learn to deal with sensory situations they must encounter as adults someday, seems cruel to me. I have actually witnessed such a situation and the end result was the child going into a full blown meltdown. I have complete empathy for that child because I have tried repeatedly to "train" myself to endure shopping during the busy holiday season (to no avail) by using a script complete with navigational maps, communication phrases, and back up plans for everything from an out of stock item to running into someone who knows you and wants to chat. The totality of the large mass of people squeezing themselves down crowded aisles, the pungent smell of overly used perfumes and colognes, the same Christmas music playing over and over again, and the noise and flashing tree lights increases my anxiety level to the point where after just a few short minutes I end up running out of the store in a panic mode every time.

I live in a small town with only one major department-like store. Even if I don't shop for Christmas presents I will still have to frequent the store during holiday season to purchase regular household commodities. To complicate matters even further I am mesmerized by colorful shiny objects. The Christmas decoration aisles teeming with a vast array of shiny tree ornaments, garlands, and tinsels act as a siren beckoning me to come closer. The power of this lure is equivalent to the power of pheromones, and I ignore caution, scripts, common sense, and the rising sensation of sensory overload just so I can stare at these objects close up. Although I am focused entirely on the ornaments it doesn't mean that my body isn't registering sensory issues. By the time I refocus back to the shopping at hand I am close to a sensory meltdown, my anxiety level is critical, and I didn't even recognize it at the time because of this narrow focus.

Avoidance of shopping is not an alternative but I have to realize my limitations that can't be dismissed. I have learned to compromise. I shop when there is a greater probability of low people volume, like when the store first opens, close to closing time, and Sunday mornings when many of our local town folk are in church. When possible I ask my husband to go to the store for me and I hand him a shopping list. I am asked why I don't just use sensory reduction devices such as noise cancellation headphones, sunglasses, or a hat with a big brim to help reduce the impact of sensory triggers. Wearing such an ensemble into the store feeling and looking anxious will only serve to draw attention to me from the undercover security people looking for shoplifters. I have also found that when wearing sensory assist devices like the sunglasses and a big brimmed hat, despite my looking down at the floor to avoid seeing people, someone who knows me always ends up touching me or tapping me on the shoulder sarcastically asking if I was deliberately trying to avoid them. Then they delight in engaging in small talk about subjects I have no interest in listening to, such as their Christmas shopping plans or ideas. That subjects me to a longer exposure time to sensory triggers. As an adult, a person with high functioning forms of autism has the distinct disadvantage of looking "normal" so therefore can't be seen as autistic by society. And as I stated before, to the general population autism conjures images of individuals rocking, flagrant hand flapping, and engaging in bizarre behaviors, so any individual not engaging in such behaviors must be lying about being autistic. Even people who know I have autism will still feel slighted if I apologize and explain that I cannot chat with them at the moment due to sensory issues and then curtly say my goodbyes and walk away.

To deal with the Christmas decoration aisle issue I have a small live evergreen tree as a potted plant trimmed out with shiny garlands and colorful balls and electric lights in my parlor. It stays up all year round allowing me to "admire" it whenever I am home, thereby diminishing the craving somewhat at Christmas time to deviate from my script to view the store's Christmas displays. It is portable so if I should have visitors it can quickly be moved out of sight when out of season so that I don't "embarrass" my husband.

Luckily with today's interventions for sensory issues there are techniques that help us to cope with being in an environment that is overstimulating and children learn coping strategies to help handle many of those situations. What is sometimes overlooked, though, is the fact that all human beings have sensory limitations of one sort or another. In an attempt to normalize the child with autism, however, there is a tendency to force them to endure, even if by the technique of desensitization, environments that exceed their sensory capabilities rather than working a compromise, such as visiting a shop during non peak hours when sensory impacts would be minimal. Although every waking activity of ours revolves around scripts, sensory issues can completely dominate and ruin even the best devised script. Remember it is not about what the shoppers will think about you or your autistic child; it is about successfully navigating a life skill task without having a catastrophic reaction. Know your individual's limitations and work within them and attempt to override them for society's benefit. It is O.K. to be different in today's world.

Growing up undiagnosed with autism

Seeing as I was diagnosed as an adult with autism I am frequently asked how I managed to grow up without any formal professional interventions. Did I follow scripts and what happened when scripts weren't followed? I consider myself very fortunate, having been only diagnosed in 2005 at age 44. I was born with autism and early home movie footage shows that at age two I was already engaging in very prominent stimming. I reached those early childhood development milestones rather slowly but by age three my vocabulary just exploded and I was not only bilingual but acted as a translator between my mother, who spoke very little English, and my father, who didn't speak German. My mother is quick to say that I was a good child but just "stubborn, set in my ways, quirky, but able to spend hours entertaining myself playing with the same toy." Looking back now it is easy to see why. My mother was born before World War II into an aristocratic wealthy family and raised me in traditional German culture. She had non breakable routines, used scripts, schedules, was very punctual, and I was taught formal etiquette where I always addressed individuals by their title such as "Mrs. Smith," or "Aunt Gisela." Everything was black and white, concrete. I referred to my parents as "mother" or "father," not mommy or daddy. Back in the 1960s the German people were more reserved and stoic. Emotions weren't something that was displayed in front of others. Every aspect of daily life was regimented, scripted, and very punctual.

I remember being around six years old and watching my mother doing laundry and asking her why she ironed towels, pillow cases, and undergarments. I was told it was a "rule" taught to her by her mother, therefore something that must be followed. There were a lot of time-honored child rearing non negotiable rules imposed on me. I like to say somewhat jokingly, "I know there is a God because if you have to grow up being undiagnosed as autistic the ideal parent who would somewhat understand our needs would be a German one." What was culturally instilled in my mother translated into an environment where I flourished, and was seen as "normal." Being raised German was as close to being raised autistic as possible in a non autistic dominant world.

I had no behavioral issues until I entered kindergarten when it became mandatory to integrate with other children and accept social customs considered the norm. About the only time my behavior became explosive at home revolved around feeding times when I was still a baby. My mother delights in recalling the time I taught her about attention to details. I was about one year old and the routine for breakfast consisted of putting me in the high chair at the same time every morning and immediately serving me my porridge. It was always the same breakfast with the same apple sauce on the side. It was what I liked so my mother never felt the need to "push" different breakfast choices. This one time my mother accidentally made my cereal too hot to eat but didn't notice it till after she placed me in the high chair. Obviously not wanting to scald my mouth, she refrained from placing the bowl on the high chair tray and began to blow on it in front of me to cool it down. This breach of what in my brain became to me a routine was traumatizing. It wasn't that I was tantruming but I didn't understand why there was such an abrupt "change" in my being fed breakfast. She went off script. I began wailing, screaming, and flailing my limbs all around me. My poor mother desperately tried, in vain, to hurry cooling down the cereal. Twenty minutes later my "outburst" had me so worked up that I turned beet red and was unable to breathe, therefore unable to eat breakfast at all. She said after that "incident" she always paid attention to the little "details" and made sure never to put me in the high chair till the food was ready to be served. Other than incidents where she realized there was a break in structure or routine she claims I was a model child albeit set in my own ways. The issue wasn't that I was acting willfully, but that my script and routine were interrupted.

Dispelling the myth that non verbal individuals with autism must possess low cognitive function, I cannot stress enough that whether someone is verbal or non verbal the thought processing is the same, so this book is applicable to the entire autism spectrum and not just to the higher functioning and/or Asperger's Syndrome group. A child or adult with autism who is non verbal may not be able to "talk" to us using the spoken word but they communicate their frustration through behavior. All behaviors are a form of communication. I still encounter within the general population the belief that non verbal individuals with autism have low I.Q.s and minimal, if any, reasoning capabilities. The contents of this book will enlighten those of you who interact with anyone on the autism spectrum, whether severely autistic or very high functioning.

"Scripting": the golden rule in autism

It is important that you the reader understand what I have coined as the "golden rule of all people with autism," as it directly clashes with the non autistic mindset. This rule is something all individuals with autism follow whether they are aware of it or not. Simply stated the golden rule is: "We need every second of every minute of every hour scripted."

Anyone who has encountered an event where something went off script for an autistic individual, unplanned or otherwise, will surely tell you it didn't go smoothly. We have this compelling need for order as well as an intense drive to structure our day into timetables or schedules. We create "scripts" of how the day or event is to unfold according to an orderly plan that we devise in our head. Unfortunately, though this plan is flawless in our minds we don't seem to communicate that plan to those around us until it collides with a non autistic agenda. Living in a dominantly non autistic world that seems to thrive on spontaneity is almost incomprehensible to a person with autism. The natural world isn't chaotic or random, it is orderly, predictable, and adheres to a predetermined timetable (or as I like to view it, "script"). The natural order of things dictates that we are born, live a life span, and then die. To break this routine, script, or order of things would result in absolute chaos and severe mental anguish, as succinctly portrayed in every zombie movie ever produced. Even seemingly unpredictable random weather events like thunderstorms follow strict patterns governing weather such as fronts, air masses, clouds, etc. To us changing the natural order of things we are used to is as distressing as waking up one morning and suddenly finding out the world has been taken over by zombies.

GOING OFF SCRIPT

Going off script is equally as terrifying as jumping out of an airplane without a parachute. Why is it so terrifying? Is it a fear of the unknown?

If so, why then when someone tries to explain to a person with autism that a change is just about to occur and what to expect, is there either still strong opposition to this abrupt change or intense negative reaction. Reassuring phrases such as "Don't worry, it's taken care of," or "It will be fine" offer little if any consolation.

In a nutshell it is about losing control of our immediate environment where things can happen that we have no script for. It is a primal need for safety, and we manipulate the environment around us to achieve predictability because of this intense anxiety of the unforeseen. This dominates our every waking moment. Going off script is losing control and losing control puts us at the mercy of "chance" which is random, unpredictable, and offers no sense of self security. We script to feel safe. This starts at an early age even if the child is unaware of why they are doing it. Scripting to navigate our way through today's society becomes even more critical because we have to counterbalance how today's society doesn't even follow its own scripts or take into consideration how breaking their's affects us. Case in point is going for a doctor's visit. How many times have you had an appointment for say 11:00 am and you end up waiting 45 minutes before being seen just because there are a lot of patients that day? I have witnessed quite a few fellow patients getting upset and complaining to the receptionist that their wait time is affecting their schedule and they have to be either back at work, or picking up the kids, or at other appointments they can't miss. I see their frustration and I have empathy for them, for this is what it feels like for us when we go off script. The anxiety that accompanies this feeling seems to cast a sense of doom and gloom over the remaining day because the predictability that we had predetermined in our brains by careful scripting has been shattered and we are out of control of our environment. I cannot emphasize enough how paramount scripting of everything from major events to daily life skills such as meal time or bedtime routines is critical to our sense of well being and if you are the one doing the scripting you cannot deviate from that once it has been communicated to the individual. Let me give you a perfect example of a very common easily overlooked breach of staying on the script you created for the child with autism.

Let's say you are in the process of preparing dinner, which will be macaroni and cheese and find that there isn't enough cheese for the dish. Seeing as the grocery store isn't that far away you decide to "run to the store" to pick up the needed ingredient. Since there is no one else who can watch your autistic child, who we will call "Timmy," it is obvious he will have to accompany you to the store. To a non autistic child it is easy to say, "Come on, Timmy, get your coat, we have to go to the store to get a few things." Other than some possible protesting about not wanting to leave his preferred activity Timmy generally complies. If Timmy is autistic, however, usually a phrase like that will result in what I call the "But what if?" syndrome.

It starts with, "Come on, Timmy, get your coat, we have to go to the store to get some cheese for dinner." Typically the conversation will unfold like this: Timmy starts right in with, "But what if we get to an intersection and there is road construction and we get detoured and you get lost?"

You reply by telling him you know another route to get there. He then asks, "But what if we get to the store and find that they don't have the cheese you want?" Again you tell him that you would buy a comparable brand or type of cheese that would not affect the quality of the dinner. Timmy is growing visibly more anxious with every response to his questions.

He becomes relentless, asking numerous "But what if?" questions. Many mothers have told me that they feel Timmy is just stalling because he doesn't want to go to the store. While this may be a tactic employed by non autistic children it is not so for the autistic child who is desperately communicating to you that they need more scripting for this trip to the grocery store. The "But what if?"s even if they seem far-fetched to you, convey his need to plan and script various potential scenarios that logically could occur even, if only as a remote possibility, so that he has alternate scripts he can count on as a back up plan should your script be altered by the unforeseen. Timmy doesn't feel safe even in your presence without these back up scripts because he doesn't know how you would respond to going off script unless you communicate that upfront with him before you set off on the excursion. Despite your best intentions you can't pre-script everything perfectly and there will be times when scripts don't go according to plan. Taking the time to allow Timmy to ask his "But what if?" questions will serve to calm him down because scripting is one of our major coping strategies for dealing with the non autistic world. It makes us feel somewhat safe and in control even when we are in a situation that is out of control. It is a natural part of autistic childhood development where we begin to develop the skills that will create coping strategies for the unpredictable events that life will throw at us as adults by having alternate scripts to fall back on in just such a case.

To ease the "But what if?" syndrome try communicating the anticipated event succinctly and clearly. Let's rephrase the announcement of having to go to the store in such a way Timmy isn't compelled to grill you with 101 questions. This is how the conversation should unfold in such a way that Timmy has a workable script that has been clearly defined and spelled out for him by you:

> Timmy, I have to go to the store to buy some cheese. I was gathering all the ingredients for tonight's meal preparation and I realized I needed two cups of shredded

cheddar cheese and I only have one cup left in the package, which is not enough. There is no one else here to watch you while I am gone so you must accompany me to the grocery store. We will get our jackets from the closet and put them on because it is cold outside. You will sit in the front seat next to me in the car. We will go down our street, turn right onto Main Street, and follow that 2.3 miles till we reach the grocery store I always shop at. After parking the car you and I will proceed into the store, walk down the bakery aisle all the way back to the dairy case where they keep the cheese. I will pick out a package of cheddar cheese needed to complete the two cups called for in the recipe. This store always carries on hand many different brands of the shredded cheese we need so it is highly unlikely they will not have what I need. Should, however, this be the case my back up plan will be to pick up a brick of cheddar cheese and shred the cheese myself on our cheese grater when we return home. Seeing as we are in the dairy section I will also pick up a carton of milk and a dozen eggs because we only have enough of both ingredients at home to make breakfast for three days and our weekly grocery shopping day is five days away. We should be back home within the hour unless there is heavy traffic but bring your (use your child's favorite stim tool that calms them down when they get anxious) Darth Vader action figure just in case our timeframe goes over one hour due to unforeseen road construction detours.

This will go a long way to minimizing the "But what if?" questions because you scripted in the details in such a way that Timmy now has a working visual in his mind of how the trip will unfold and what to expect. But please don't commit the following most common mistake: "You know, while I am here I might as well just grab a shopping cart and pick up a few other things." Almost instantly Timmy's anxiety level sky rockets and he becomes visibly distressed. Why? It is because you went off script. You said you were only going to the store to buy three things: cheese, eggs, and milk, and now you have altered this script by deciding to shop for other items. This impulsive decision then creates a domino effect where every element of the original script also changes in essence, leaving little Timmy without a working script which destroys his inner sense of control and feeling safe. Timmy had a mental picture of just how long it would take to reach the dairy case, what aisles would be traversed, using the express check-out lane requiring ten items or fewer, which is much quicker than the regular check-out lanes, driving home before the rush hour begins, and an overall timeframe of one hour or less. Now how can he revise this script on such short notice? He has to contemplate how much longer will we be in the store shopping for the other items. Will there be more than ten items, which will force us to use the regular check-out lanes which are usually very busy with shoppers pushing shopping carts overflowing with hundreds of food items, and who have a tendency to utilize the slowest check-writing skills imaginable, which serves to further delay our exiting the store? Will this extra time translate into driving home during rush hour? If so, how much longer will this supposedly one hour or less trip last?

He may understand that sometimes going off script for unforeseeable reasons is the reality of life but in this case you, his mom, just completely disregarded his need for predictability, destroying his inner sense of preservation, and without the working script which you spelled out to him before leaving the house he is literally lost. Timmy understands this going off script was a choice made without forewarning him and not an event beyond his mom's control. A sense of helplessness will set in, creating a tendency to lash out verbally or behaviorally out of desperation. Deciding to shop for a few more items may seem like only a minor infraction of a predetermined script to someone without autism but to us going off script anywhere in the script is just as unnerving, whether it is being broadsided while driving by another vehicle or having Mom decide to add in some last minute shopping. To Timmy it is earth shattering.

Our need to script is one of our core traits that we cannot eliminate or diminish the importance of. You will never go wrong by explaining in detail what is to unfold clearly, succinctly, and with contingencies added. It will go a long way in gaining our trust and having us feel relaxed around you.

HATING SPONTANEITY

There are many reasons why we prefer to be more solitary creature than social butterfly but one is our distrust of being around non autistic individuals because they are spontaneous, willing to sometimes "go with the flow," alter plans midstream, and generally don't mind not adhering to agreed upon timetables. During my teen years I made several attempts to establish friendships with other girls my age. The early 1970s heralded the invention of large indoor shopping malls compared to the individual stores congregated in a plaza. It became the socially accepted norm for teenage girls to spend their free time shopping at the mall. I have accompanied different female peers on numerous outings and social functions where they decided on an impromptu side trip to the mall in search of just one article of clothing before continuing on to our activity. I was always told, "This won't take long." I believed them because we agreed upon an arrival time to whatever function we were going to that night and I wanted to fit in with my peers socially so I subjected myself to their whims. Without fail they always seemed to lose track of time and constantly we ended up arriving late. To complicate matters further they would have to explore each clothes rack just out of curiosity.

My script for shopping tends to be more of a mission with a specific target in mind with no deviations. If I need a new shirt I go into the store straight to the racks that offer shirts, look for the section that carries my size, and I thumb through the available section. I like to wear similar styles and colors so if that rack contains nothing that I want I exit the store. It seems senseless to "browse" the aisles in hopes of seeing something that may act as a substitute. In the company of these girls I would grow increasingly distressed over timeframes that now did not match the arrival time for the function we originally agreed upon. This ruined my script so badly I could not enjoy the evening because I could not overcome the late arrival and subsequently I became very distrustful going with anyone anywhere because I could not count on them staying on time.

Even to this day, whenever possible my non autistic husband and I will take separate vehicles when attending the same social function because despite our predetermining a set time to leave he may be having such a good time at a party that he wants to stay beyond our allotted time, or he may take too long to get ready before we leave for the event, causing us to be late. My need to follow a script is so intense that in order to avoid a scene over this, because I get very visibly anxious rapidly (it is obvious to everyone around me), we take separate vehicles, which means my script stays intact even if he changes his. About the only time I feel comfortable going someplace with another person is if we are taking separate vehicles. It is all about staying on script and the lengths we go to to ensure that.

DEALING WITH GOING OFF SCRIPT

It is important to realize that we will all have the unexpected happen to us in life that takes us off script and sometimes back up scripts will fail, so having an immediate calming tool available to handle the anxiety will help us deal with calming the raging sense of helplessness we feel when our scripts fail. Non autistic people are no different from autistic people in this regard because they also use various "tools" to calm their anxiety when faced with the unexpected. Have you ever found yourself commuting home from work on a Friday evening and running into a complete traffic standstill because of someone else's auto accident up ahead that caused the highway you were traveling on to be closed until the emergency medical services vehicles arrived? With no exits close by you are stuck waiting it out without any workable timeframe of when traffic will be allowed past the accident site. How do you handle your frustration and anxiety in that situation? Some commuters will turn the radio on to a station that plays relaxing music, others may take out a book to read while enduring the wait (I have actually seen people in neighboring autos read the newspaper when I was in this situation), still others may light up a cigarette. They are all calming tools very similar to our use of stim tools to ease anxiety when faced with unforeseen events.

It is important that little Timmy should understand at an early age that while scripting is very beneficial in helping us deal with daily life there will be times when things don't go as planned, so it is of the utmost importance to have a calming technique available for those times when we can't remedy the problem and must just endure it. Wailing and flailing limbs in this situation will not make him feel any less anxious and is socially unacceptable in public, especially as an adult. I have seen non autistic drivers in vehicles around me get so enraged because their timetable was interrupted by the highway accident that they constantly beep their horns, shout obscenities, and make obscene hand gestures to anyone glancing their way. That is also totally socially unacceptable and perhaps if they became more autistic-like and used calming stim tools, like the socially popular stress balls you can squeeze or worry stones to rub in the palm of your hand, it might decrease the incidents of road rage plaguing our roadways.

The point is that, understanding how important scripting is to our inner sense of well being, every autistic individual should brace themselves for going off intended scripts through no fault of their own frequently throughout life, and prepare for them by having calming tools on hand to use in these circumstances when there is no alternate script to fall back on. I am an individual who once behind the wheel of a vehicle begins to fret over possible but highly unlikely scenarios that would cause me to be late in my expected arrival time before I even leave the driveway. I have a GPS navigational system which gives me an estimated arrival time as well as alternate routes should the one I plan on be detoured due to road construction, or I take a wrong turn, or I am unsure of the directions. It helps in reducing the anxiety of unforeseen circumstances, but I carry a road atlas as well just in case the GPS system malfunctions or is out of satellite range as a back-up script to follow. With new roads being added frequently and old ones changing names even road atlases become outdated and inaccurate quickly. Despite having both of these countermeasures I have on occasion found myself hopelessly lost trying to find my final destination point, whether due to erroneous directions, auto accidents, or road detours.

For times such as these when my back-up scripts fail and I feel a sense of panic for going off my timetable I carry a special CD to play that calms me down. Gregorian chanting is very calming when I feel anxious. Somehow just the tone of the chant seems to ease the mental anguish I am experiencing. I don't play it regularly as that will over time desensitize me to the calming effect it offers. I have such a CD in every vehicle I drive, and I carry one with me when I am a passenger in someone else's vehicle, along with a portable CD player with headphones so I don't bother the driver with my music should I need to resort to it. Because I am stressed when faced with an unscripted driving occurrence and not in control when someone else is driving I don't want to "share" my music with others in the vehicle. I want to listen to it uninterrupted to calm down and I like the volume high enough to drown out all extraneous noises so all my brain registers is the soothing music. Headphones allow for that. Playing that CD when someone else is driving at a volume low enough where one can talk over the music can aggravate the anxiety I am experiencing with something as benign as the comment, "That is really pretty music," because it interrupts my concentration on internally calming myself down. I have found that, at least as an adult, when I am in a stressed out situation in the presence of someone else they feel obligated to attempt to calm me down with reassuring phrases that only incite my anxiety such as, "Don't worry, this too shall pass," or try to divert my focus onto something requiring thought, which is too demanding on me at that moment. Blocking everything out, including people, to focus on Gregorian chanting allows my brain to decompress and function more clearly. For me it isn't an option but a requirement when driving scripts go awry. I have many tools and techniques to utilize when faced with various other script malfunctions.

Realize that when we are working on self calming techniques we need to be able to focus on gaining control of our anxiety without the distraction of someone trying to converse with us at that moment unless we initiate conversation. Help your child with autism begin to recognize what calming tools and/or techniques work for those times when things go off script, and they will have to endure through the unscripted situation. Have whatever special stim tool or calming technique that works for your child available in the vehicle so that they can self soothe when the unforeseen occurs and things go off script. It is the goal of every parent of an autistic child to be able to have their child self regulate their behaviors in public as an adult. Going off any script can cause explosive, even rage-like behaviors, if distressing enough, so it is important to help the child understand that things in life will not always go as scripted and they must learn to cope with the help of stim tools or calming techniques when scripts fail.

CHAPTER 2

Anxiety: Friend or Foe?

The most frequently asked question I receive revolves around the issue of whether a child with autism would benefit from being placed on anti-anxiety medication. To the non autistic individual it appears that autistic individuals live in a near constant state of anxiety even when in an environment that is non stressful.

Neurological makeup similar to certain animal species

We have an overactive or heightened fight or flight response. When out of our autistic comfort zone we tend to be hypervigilant, fidgety, unable to relax, constantly fretting about things that may possibly (even if highly improbably) go wrong. Being startled can trigger a bolting response. Anxiety is a natural state for us because it is part of our neurological makeup. Individuals with autism tend to have a heightened fight or flight response very similar in neurological characteristics to that in non predatory animal species like deer, cattle, sheep, and horses, especially herd animals. Individuals with autism often have an almost uncanny ability to communicate and relate successfully to animals while at the same time experiencing great difficulties in communicating with people. These are the children who can spot objects of interest off in the distance through the corner of their eye well before the individual accompanying them can; the children who seem to lack space boundary awareness by getting too close to other people's faces while attempting to communicate something they deem important. It is almost a contradiction that many individuals on the spectrum find light touch aversive yet enjoy deep pressure touch. To fully appreciate the role of anxiety in autism it should be examined in context to the overall parallel of similar neurological responses in certain species of animals. I have spoken with hundreds of parents, caregivers, professionals, and people with autism of all ages who share this same concept. Understand that the natural instinctual characteristics that I will discuss throughout this book are influenced by outside environmental forces such as home life, economic status, and cultural expectations. Just because you may not see traits I discuss in this chapter in the individual you are working with doesn't mean that they don't exist. All autistic individuals are just that; individuals with different strengths and limitations. Not everyone will experience every single characteristic of autism or for that matter the same responses to anxiety. While the fight or flight response is similar in every person on the spectrum the degree to which it manifests itself will vary from individual to individual. It is simply an instinctual reaction to the external environment and not learned behavior.

Difficulty making eye contact

Let's start with eye contact, or lack of eye contact. The ability or inability to make eye contact should never be a defining characteristic ruling autism in or out as a diagnosis. There will be some individuals on the spectrum who have no difficulty sustaining eye contact but are no less autistic than another individual with autism who cannot make eye contact. There are three main reasons (the first not relating to animals) why making or sustaining eye contact is so difficult.

REASON 1: SENSORY INTEGRATION

First, most individuals with autism cannot process sensory input from more than one sense at a time. This is referred to as sensory integration difficulty, the most common of which is an inability to process auditory and visual input simultaneously. If you have ever asked an autistic individual to "Look at me when I am talking to you," you have unknowingly asked them to interpret information from two different senses at the same time. If they do have sensory integration difficulties then this seemingly simple request becomes an impossible task to complete. So much emphasis is being placed on teaching eye contact that it has become almost mandatory, despite our inability to process sensory input from two sources at the same time. Even with successful training where the individual can sustain eye contact when someone is talking to them, if they have sensory integration issues in this area then they will not be able to hear every word and will have difficulty fully comprehending what is being said. I have had the opportunity to converse with hundreds of individuals on the spectrum, many of whom had had formal training in sustaining eye contact. It was easy to spot the individuals with this type of sensory integration difficulty. Although they made eye contact their overall affect was tense, rigid, and speech seemed slower, stilted, and calculated. Most had difficulty sustaining prolonged conversation due to concentration and focusing abilities. Since I cannot sustain eye contact very long myself I would just briefly express this to them as I looked away. With sighs of relief just about every person I spoke with expressed the same difficulty. Dropping the formality of eye contact our conversations then became animated, relaxed, and fulfilling. The non autistic individuals who accompanied them were always amazed at how they "opened up" speaking with me and would ask what strategy I used to do this. There was and is no magic strategy; I just didn't force what I knew they (and I) could not naturally overcome.

Some autistic individuals can make eye contact without any apparent difficulties. These individuals could still have sensory integration issues but with other sensory processes. American society is overly obsessed with eye contact, erroneously assuming a lack of it infers deceit, guilt, or disinterest. Non autistic individuals who make and sustain eye contact can be very deceitful or guilty even while looking directly into another person's eyes, thereby nullifying eye contact as a means of determining honesty. I recommend that if eye contact is a goal that is very difficult to master for the individual you are working or relating with then allow them the freedom of understanding and conversing with others without requiring eye contact. I have numerous sensory integration difficulties. When I have to converse with someone for any length of time I don't apologize for being autistic, explaining that my lack of eye contact is a deficit associated with this "disability." That implies I am handicapped and not a fully functioning member of society, plus in a society that still harbors major misconceptions of autism I do not prefer to disclose to everyone I meet that I am autistic. It is no one's business but my own. I have learned to confidently briefly state a reason for not sustaining eye contact if the conversation becomes extended or requires my undivided attention. I simply say, "I just want you to know upfront that although I am looking down at the floor while you are speaking I am hearing every word you say. I have visual and auditory integration difficulties that make sustaining eye contact extremely difficult."

I have used this line thousands of times and not once did I encounter a single person who became offended at my lack of eye contact. I find it humorous while conducting my seminars on autism that the attendees will nod in agreement and pledge to not to force auditory and sensory integration if it is too difficult but quickly forget this important concept. I am always asked during breaks or afterwards to sign autographs which I gladly do but more often than not I am asked, "Can I ask you a question while you are signing my book?" That is something I cannot do with sensory integration difficulties because it requires me to think and write as well as listen carefully and try to process what they are saying simultaneously.

The school system will encounter many behaviors, perhaps even explosive ones, if sensory processing issues aren't acknowledged. Besides the lack of required eye contact another commonly overlooked sensory integration trigger is having to copy notes that the teacher is writing on the chalkboard while at the same time listening to what she is lecturing about. I remember as a child getting so frustrated with trying to listen and copy notes from the chalkboard because without fail I would only have half of her notes copied before she erased the notes to move on in her lesson. I became anxious because I could not keep up with the rest of class in understanding the lesson properly and by the afternoon periods I would make audible noises out of frustration. Being continually reprimanded for such vocalizations led to very defiant behavior. I eventually just didn't bother to pay attention in class at all, opting to learn the material solely out of the school book at home. I begged my mother daily to allow me to stay home and forgo school, to no avail. How sad that throughout my entire school career I was labeled a behavioral problem due to defiant or non compliant attitudes when in reality it was mainly due to sensory integration and processing difficulties.

There should be no feelings of guilt when an autistic person offers a brief explanation of not making eye contact but still listening attentively to someone when wanting to converse with them. It is not about making excuses but stating reasonable accommodations for our neurological processing differences with confidence and not apologetically. I understand the need to ensure that children with autism learn ways to adapt and fit into our society but so much emphasis is placed on forcing children on the autism spectrum to become "normal" that some well meaning goals will be unrealistic and fraught with much frustration. At some point the non autistic world has to meet us half way, and beginning with the acceptance of the inability to make eye contact is a great start to true integration with society.

REASON 2: PERIPHERAL VERSUS CENTRAL VISION

The second reason for a lack of direct eye contact is related to herd animals. It has to do with visual fields. Did you ever notice that herd animal species, such as horses, cows, goats, sheep, deer, and elk, for example, have eyes on the side of their head? This is a survival mechanism allowing for great peripheral fields of vision so as to be able to spot predators that may be stalking them at a distance. Unfortunately, because the eye sockets are set at opposite sides of the skull these animals have "blind spots" in front of their face meaning they cannot see directly in front of them. Their central vision is severely hindered. I have a small herd of horses and ponies. Besides riding I spend countless hours feeding, grooming, and handling each one so they know me intimately. Still I am careful when I approach any one of them from directly in front because they will have a tendency to become startled and instinctually shy backwards due to the surprise element of my close proximity. Predatory animals like tigers; raptors such as falcons, eagles, and owls; bears, wolves, and many others have eyes in front of the skull which makes them extremely proficient with central vision allowing them to focus clearly on every movement of the prey that they are stalking.

If you are a professional or parent of a non verbal child you are familiar with how they initiate interaction with their teacher or caregiver. It is natural for them to approach you not directly from the front but generally coming alongside of you instead. I was once observing a six-year-old non verbal child in the classroom setting because I was called in to consult on frequent meltdowns he had during the school day. For the first two hours he totally ignored my presence despite my sitting at his work table. Once he felt comfortable with my being there he became curious and wanted to interact with me using hand gestures he had learned. He positioned himself directly to my side and then reached out to touch my shoulder with his hand. Without turning to look at him I acknowledged his opening a dialog, so to speak. He immediately sat down by my side and began to utilize hand gestures as a means of communication. His teacher quickly attempted to reposition him so he was sitting in front of me so we could "see each other," resulting in the boy becoming severely agitated and anxious. I told her to just allow the boy the freedom to communicate in a relaxed manner, which he did while by my side. This same child could when entering a room see some special object of interest in the farthest area just through the corner of his eyes. Even if he held an object of interest he would "stare" at it by holding it off more to his side than directly in front of him. Just like herd animals he had a highly developed peripheral visual field. I see this very often when observing interactions in non verbal individuals. While I do not know of any official clinical research studies done on this subject I have in my personal interactions with individuals, their families, and providers observed and discussed this peripheral visual field and all have agreed with my insight (or scientific speculation due to a lack of professional studies). The easiest way to determine whether my theory applies to your individual is to try this simple strategy. Instead of sitting directly in front of the person, try sitting off to their side or diagonally across when interacting with them. Watch their reaction. If they seem to relax and be more in tune with you then it may have a predominantly peripheral field of view.

Mothers have confided in me, saying, "You know some of the best relaxed conversations I have ever had with my Asperger's child have been when I am driving the vehicle and my child is sitting in the front seat next to me." Again, just like herd animals and non verbal individuals high functioning autistics tend to have excellent peripheral vision with poorly developed central vision. These are the children, verbal and non verbal, who will hold the book, object of interest, or hand held video game very close to their face. These children seem to have atrocious handwriting, and will sit extremely close to the television set. The most common social faux pas these individuals commit is getting too close to other people when communicating, almost "in their face" literally and figuratively. Why is it that little autistic Timmy when he has something of real importance to tell you or wants your complete undivided attention gets his face so close to yours that he is almost touching you? It is *not* on most occasions a space boundary issue but a visual field issue. Because many of us have peripheral vision as our primary field of view we cannot see well directly in front of us.

Books have been written on the fact that people with autism lack facial recognition. In a lot of the information on autism I have read autistic adults who cannot look into another person's face are quoted as complaining that "it hurts physically" to do so, or that all they see is snow or static and they cannot make out facial features. It hurts physically because it requires the eyes to focus in a way they are not accustomed to. Try gazing cross eyed at an object a few inches in front of your face for five minutes. Chances are that after just a few moments it will become tiresome and physically painful because your eyes have not been used to focusing on objects in that manner. Anything relatively directly in front of us like a person standing will be out of focus while right behind them or off to the sides the view is crystal clear. The only way we can truly utilize our central vision is by blocking out peripheral fields by instinctively bringing the object extremely close to our face so that everything else around us is unseen. I have great empathy for the thousands of poor little autistic children reprimanded for space boundary infractions when in many instances all they are attempting to do is to see the person clearly and give them their undivided attention. With primary peripheral vision we tend to become easily distracted by things going on around the individual we are supposed to be paying attention to. Sometimes sudden movements in the background cause a startle response. The child may then be wrongly perceived as a hyperactive child with an attention deficit. Primary peripheral vision can, in fact, be an asset when harnessed properly.

I have throughout my adult years always belonged to volunteer search and rescue units. Currently I am a captain in the United States Air Force Auxiliary as a ground search and rescue team leader. Those who know me, including my family, nicknamed me "Eagle Eye Lipsky" because I can spot objects of interest faster than those around me by scanning the area with my highly developed peripheral vision. In search and rescue missions when we are looking for a lost and/or injured person or a plane crash in the wilderness I can scan an area in half the time of someone else and be able to spot the minutest of details that are out of place in that environment which could be clues to the search. I can spot a coin on the floor yards away without even looking, so to speak, but if I happen to drop a pencil on the floor directly in front of me I cannot find it unless I move away, putting distance between myself and the fallen pencil so that I can "scan" (utilize my peripheral field to its best advantage) the area to retrieve the writing implement.

While not totally responsible for the inability to read non verbal body language I am convinced that a lot of the subtle body cues and gestures we tend not to pick up on may be a direct result of not seeing the person in full clarity. If I stand at a reasonable distance away from another while conversing and the face appears very blurry how can I expect to notice subtle facial gestures such as the raising of an eyebrow, a smile, scowl, or a wink?

Exercises to improve central vision

There are eye exercises one can implement to help develop a better central field of view. One I recommend because I have used it on myself is to take an object of interest and hold it up close to the person's face. Ask them to focus on that object. Then gradually move the object back and forth in a straight line, slowly going a little farther away each time, for no more than a couple of minutes at a time. Over time it will perhaps increase central vision accuracy. You will be able to tell if it is working by observing if the individual starts placing objects they used to hold close to their eyes further away, for instance a book. In my case it has improved my central vision when I am working on "close up" tasks such as threading a sewing needle, gluing a broken piece of pottery back together, or counting coins, for example, but overall I find myself using peripheral vision as my primary field of view.

REASON 3: A NON AGGRESSIVE GESTURE

Even if you can get the person to override the two reasons mentioned above for poor eye contact you will have a third reason or hurdle to contend with. As in animals with similar instinctual fight or flight responses eye contact is interpreted as a sign of aggression and a lack of eye contact communicates a non aggressive encounter. Whether an individual with autism is conscious of this fact or not, direct eye contact towards us creates an inner sense of uneasiness that will tend to increase to the point where this uneasiness transforms into anxiety if prolonged. Just as in animals this inner "feeling" is a primal warning mechanism, part of the fight or flight response triggered by the brain perceiving direct eye contact as a threat.

Light touch interpreted as aversive

Another animal connection through the heightened fight or flight response revolves around light touch. Why do the majority of autistic individuals find light touch very distressing? Sensory overload issues may in part trace back to the heightened fight or flight response. Human skin contains nerve receptors that sense and communicate back to the brain sensations it encounters, such as pain from a paper cut or the tickling of a cat's whiskers as the animal brushes up against a bare leg. It would make sense that in a person with heightened senses these sensations would be greatly intensified.

Being around horses for close to 40 years I have observed how something as simple as the unexpected light touch of a palm can unnerve these creatures. If you approach a horse from his blind spot or come upon him unaware and then gently place your hand on his rump, more often than not this response startles him and he instinctively pulls away from the sensation. This is a survival mechanism designed to protect the horse from being attacked and brought down by a predator from behind or from outside their field of view. Even if my horses are in their stanchion stalls eating grain while I am doing barn chores all around them, they have a tendency to startle if lightly touched anywhere from the mid section back. It is good horsemanship to always warn the animal that you are approaching them from behind and touch them firmly along either side first, where they are apt to have you in their field of view, before stepping directly behind their rump, especially when the horse is preoccupied with eating. The very first lesson anyone learns when being around horses is to never walk behind or stand behind a horse within striking distance of their hind legs. When I visit horses that don't know me or when I try to calm a nervous horse by reassuringly patting them on their neck, their tendency is to startle. All horses have an instinctual heightened fight or flight response and despite the best training in the world will engage in a "knee jerk" reaction if startled for any reason. This includes horses deemed so safe and predictable for the inexperienced rider they are often referred to as being "bomb proof," especially when focusing on something relaxing like grazing in a meadow or eating grain. Their nervous system is wired to be ready at a moment's notice to flee from a predatory attack and heightened nerve receptors in the skin interprets light touch as the first sensation of a predatory attack signaling the brain to flee.

I strongly feel that the same applies to autism. With our fight or flight response naturally heightened the brain interprets any light touch as a danger signal. This accounts for the aversion to light touch but not for the deep pressure touch we so often crave. Deep pressure touch is calming because you are actually compressing those overly sensitive nerve endings to the point of blocking their transmission of a danger signal to the brain. It relaxes us because our body can momentarily suspend the constant physiological state of hypervigilance. It is not my intent to minimize the importance of using sound sensory integration strategies to help in this area, such as body brushing, but I cannot stress enough that even with desensitization techniques you are dealing with instinctual responses that may be subdued with sensory therapies but will resurface, sometimes intensely, when the individual becomes overly stressed.

The fight or flight response

It is no wonder that many children and adults on the spectrum seem to bond so well with animals. I feel like a kindred spirit with animals because I can identify with how they react when taken by surprise. I also appreciate the need to script my movements in such a way as not to appear aggressive towards the animal through slow methodical body gestures. I like to tell people you will do well communicating with autistic individuals if you think of us as the neighbor's new puppy. You approach this puppy very slowly, extending your hand out towards them, allowing them to draw near when feeling safe to sniff your hand. Your voice is low and soothing and every movement seems almost exaggerated in its execution. Sometimes children in this situation get so excited they may run towards the puppy screeching in delight causing the puppy to react in fear by either running away or cowering behind an object. We are the puppy.

Quick sudden movements or loud boisterous speech coming our way, no matter who it is, instinctually sets off the fight or flight response. I have found myself on more than one occasion trying to purchase something in the store only to have a woman recognize me from a distance. It is usually an acquaintance or someone who attended one of my lectures who becomes excited at the prospect of being able to stop and chat with me.

This is definitely something that is gender specific, afflicting only women, and I have seen this form of unnerving behavior between other women countless times in public. From a distance she begins to squeal in delight, waving her arms furiously over her head, running towards me in anticipation of a big hug as if I were some long lost relative she just spotted. No matter how hard I try to brace myself for this encounter every fiber in my body screams at me to turn in the opposite direction and flee for my life. It is extremely difficult, if not impossible, to override these intense impulses to run away from danger. While the intent is not to frighten us, it does. Just like a terrified puppy I will run away leaving the woman bewildered over my sudden exit from the scene. For the same reasons I and many adults like myself avoid public events that tend to trigger sudden impulsive behaviors in others, such as sporting events. You can't predict when a goal or point will be scored or a great play be executed that results in spontaneous applause, jeers at the other team, or shouting out words of praise from the spectators in your proximity. All this sudden explosive stimulation encircling you 360 degrees triggers the fight or flight response, and when overstimulating translates into a panic attack you lose focus, resulting in impaired judgment.

A PREHISTORIC CARRY OVER

While self awareness of certain triggers, intense mental discipline, and manipulation of the external environment may lessen the initial intensity of a fight or flight response, it cannot be extinguished. It is part of our internal makeup. In prehistoric times primitive man was not at the top of the food chain. Our cavemen ancestors struggled daily with preventing themselves from being consumed by predators such as the saber tooth tiger. I am sure the fight or flight response in autistic individuals, heightened as it is, pales in comparison to that of our early ancestors. Gradually *Homo sapiens* did move to the top of the food chain. Soon tribes and clans merged into early civilizations and as man became urbanized this heightened survival mechanism needed to detect the danger of being hunted by other species diminished. Today, however, we still possess this fight or flight response at a barely noticeable level on a daily basis. Goose bumps that arise in all of us when frightened are actually a carried over trait of the response of primitive man. When mankind was still in its infancy both men and women had much more body hair than today. Besides helping to keep them warm, when frightened or startled the body hair bristled up much like that of a cat. A cat that is frightened or startled will bristle up the hair along its back and tail, which serves to make the cat appear much larger and more formidable than it actually is. So when frightened, even today, the body will resort to bristling up body hair as a defense mechanism, but without the body hair goose bumps are a residual trait of a once important survival mechanism.

TRIGGERING A FIGHT OR FLIGHT RESPONSE

What happens when a fight or flight response is triggered? When startled or caught off guard there are important signals that herald the onset of the fight or flight response.

1. The onset of the "freeze" response

The first sign you will notice is the "freeze"; the individual affected seems momentarily frozen in time. If ever you have stumbled upon an animal that wasn't expecting you, for instance the feral cat wandering along your fence, startled at discovering your presence, what is the first response of the cat? Does it immediately hiss and arch its back in an aggressive response or does it immediately scamper away? It does neither. The very first reaction when taken by surprise is to "freeze." This freeze doesn't last very long but it is a critical response to understand. Any animal, man included, when caught off guard and surprised will seem frozen in time even if only for a flash. A perfect example is a practical joke involving the element of surprise such as hiding in a closet and shouting "boo" when an unsuspecting person opens the closet door. Usually you will first witness a look of bewilderment accompanied by no movement, followed quickly by a reaction of screams, along with either running away or possibly striking at the individual hiding in the closet. That brief moment where the initial shock is still registering and the person seems bewildered and unable to respond is the "freeze" response.

What happens during this freeze response is critical. When suddenly frightened this instinctual response is activated. For a brief second the freeze indicates the temporary suspension of cognitive thought. The brain now switches to a purely self preservation mode and instinctually determines whether it is best to strike out or run away. During the freeze the brain is thinking, "Should I stand my ground and defend myself or should I run away from danger?" I use a simple demonstration in my seminars to illustrate this point. When I begin discussing the freeze response I wander up and down among my attendees. I try to pick out an individual who isn't paying direct attention to me and is busy writing. While speaking I let the audience know I plan to startle this individual by quietly pointing to my "target" and using the non verbal gesture of "say nothing" by placing my index finger on my lips. I walk up from behind and when standing right behind the individual I say in a loud abrupt tone, "You are not paying attention to me which is rude so I want you to leave my class!"

Without fail the attendee seems to be momentarily frozen in time (no physical movement) with such a look of bewilderment they can't speak. I wait five seconds and then say I am just kidding. I then ask the attendee to tell me what was the very first thought that came to mind when I told them to leave? Half of them said that they felt indignant over my tone and seeing as they paid good money to attend my seminar they were ready to give me "a piece of their mind," in other words confront me. The other half said they were ready to burst into tears and just grab their notebooks to hastily exit the room. The reason I asked for their initial thought is because when I startled them I triggered the fight or flight response where they reacted instantaneously and didn't have a chance to think things through. They reacted on instinct. Feeling indignant, with the mindset of "how dare she" is a fight response where the person wanted to stand their ground and confront me. The other, of wanting to exit immediately, is a flight response. It is no different for a person with autism but because we are much more hypervigilant by nature this response is magnified tenfold resulting in very dramatic behaviors.

2. The release of adrenaline

What spurs these behaviors? When the fight and flight response is triggered your body releases a sudden burst of adrenaline to give you the strength and determination to "save yourself." Chances are that if you were awakened in the middle of the night by your hotel room engulfed in flames you would automatically and instinctually immediately run out of the burning building. I seriously doubt anyone would consciously decide to pick up the phone and call a friend for advice on what to do. In news reports reporters interviewing the survivors always ask them what they were thinking when they first saw the flames or smelled smoke. In most cases the shocked survivors reply that they were too dazed to think until they were finally out of the building.

Mothers have been reported to have momentarily had herculean strength in emergencies, lifting objects many times their weight off their trapped child. It is this sudden burst of adrenaline that gives superhuman strength or shuts off the pain receptors for the sole purpose of survival. If you were to research the Congressional Medal of Honor recipients in America for heroism during war you would find many cases in which the service personnel, despite being seriously wounded, disregarded their personal welfare and committed enormous acts of bravery, saving the lives of those around them. Many recipients' family members received this medal on behalf of the fallen soldier because their actions resulted in death. Again it was the sudden release of adrenaline that not only gave them incredible strength and courage, but also temporarily diminished the pain response of their injuries.

3. Loss of cognitive awareness

In the autistic fight or flight response adrenaline also rushes through our veins once this response is triggered. This sudden burst of energy allows for running away from the situation (flight response) but unfortunately because it is instinctual the danger lies in the fact that the person is reacting and not thinking. It is during the momentary freeze that the brain switches from cognitive thinking to an instinctual self preservation reaction. If it is the flight response the overwhelming urge will be to flee. The serious danger here is the fact that they are unable to process anything and cannot recognize family members, those who work directly with them, or where they are. Our brain's only function is to get us to a place we feel safe regardless of our location. The grave consequence here is that children as well as adults will run out of buildings blindly right into traffic, and aggressively attempt to push or shove anyone standing in front of them out of their way. These individuals will be instinctually craving a safe haven devoid of sensory stimulation and will seek out dark remote places if possible. There is a tendency to find these individuals hiding in closets, under a table or bed, and in any dark cubby hole, even a cave or abandoned buildings if outdoors, to seek "safety." Dark places without sensory stimulation create an environment that is less threatening because it won't further excite them by sensory or cognitive means. It may be an extremely dangerous place, but since they are not thinking cognitively, that will elude them at that moment. It is not uncommon for someone with autism to seek a safe haven in a very dangerous environment unaware of the dangers while in this escape mode only to finally calm down, recognize they are in an unsafe environment, and then start to panic all over again.

When the flight response is triggered in an autistic person it is impossible to use reason or expect coherent interaction. Don't expect them to recognize you even if you are their parent because they can't. At this point all one can do is keep them "contained" within a safe area. I will discuss this in more detail when I discuss strategies for meltdowns later on in this book. I think the best analogy that succinctly describes our flight response is a herd of stampeding cattle.

During a stampede the animals become so frightened that their flight response is activated and they run blindly trampling anything in their path, for so intense is this self preservation mode they are just reacting on impulse. Humans are no different. Just imagine being in a crowded movie theater and someone yelling "FIRE!" and imagine the pandemonium as everyone rushes out of their seats in a blind panic trying to exit en masse. There have been countless tragedies of people either being trampled to death by others or unable to escape the burning building because the exits were so jammed with panic struck patrons. In the flight response no one had the cognitive ability to realize the door could be opened if people stopped crowding the exit and filed out in an orderly fashion.

4. The danger of injury

More people get hurt when the fight response is triggered as they attempt to restrain the autistic person who is in a full meltdown. Once again the individual is in an instinctual mode unaware of their surroundings and unable to recognize familiar faces due to cognitive shutdown. They are only able to perceive a "threat" when someone else enters their personal space. Instinctively they react by lashing out and striking this individual as a means of self preservation. Anyone who has attempted to "calm" down an escalation by trying to physically stop the individual from hitting themselves, throwing objects, or just flailing their limbs has found out the hard way that their actions only resulted in an increase in the intensity of the behaviors. These are the autistic individuals who when in a fight mode and feeling threatened display great stamina in prolonging a physical altercation with anyone who has entered their personal space and attempted to restrain them. It all comes back to this surge or burst of adrenaline coursing through their veins giving them the ability to protect themselves despite lacking cognitive thinking at that moment. Even the mild mannered child can rage into a formidable opponent during one of these fight responses and without being aware of it inflict serious bodily harm on another person entering their personal space.

For that matter an autistic person who engages in self injurious behavior during a meltdown will not only intensify that behavior if you attempt to stop them from doing it but will possibly bite, scratch, or head butt the individual trying to intervene. They feel no pain because in this fight response the pain receptors are not registering pain, as a means of self preservation. They attack the individual who is trying to intervene because they perceive the intrusion of that person into their personal space as a viable threat to their safety and life. I cannot stress enough that this is purely an instinctual response and not a willful act of retaliation during a meltdown when the fight response is triggered. During the fight or flight response is the only time where the autistic person should not be held accountable for their actions because during that event they are cognitively impaired and just reacting to stressors. At any other time such behaviors or tantrums are unacceptable and utilized as a manipulation tool to get their own way. For those times they must be held accountable but for now we are strictly dealing with instinctual responses to the fight and flight response.

The "freeze" response

Getting back to the "freeze" response manifested just prior to the fight and flight response, it is at the freeze point where you, as the intervener, have the last chance to stop a full blown meltdown. If you don't redirect and/or calm the autistic person with assurances of finding a solution to their situation during this critical phase, once the fight or flight response is engaged there is no way of averting a full blown escalation. The beginning of the freeze phase is the last window of opportunity to appeal to cognitive thought before the brain switches into instinctual survival mode. Miss that chance and all attempts to reason or talk to the individual will be futile during that time of escalation.

Unfortunately because the freeze response is quiet and subtle it often goes unnoticed by those around them. The freeze response varies from individual to individual and you can have different types of freeze responses within the same person. Know your client or child. Familiarize yourself with how they handle stress and what "signs" you notice just prior to a meltdown. Some freeze responses will be just as obvious as a startled hare that initially crouches down during a freeze phase or a deer's expression when caught in the headlights of an oncoming vehicle. Other times the response may be barely noticeable, such as when you are teaching a task to a child and all of a sudden they seem to have this far off blank stare. Many times it is misperceived as a petit mal seizure because even if you wave your hand in front of their face they are not registering your movement. It may be the result of a vague definition, use of metaphors, or non specific timeframes, just to name a few. For example, you are autistic Timmy's one on one aide. Timmy is eight years old and considered high functioning and very verbal. He comes in very excited because today is the day his class has scheduled a field trip to go to the aquarium in the afternoon. Salt water creatures are his special interest. Timmy is so excited he has difficulty staying on task, fidgets, and begins to interrupt the lesson with numerous questions regarding the type of fish there, will he be able to feed the fish, can he swim with the fishes, etc., etc. There is no ending his interrupting so finally you say in frustration, "Timmy unless you stay on task and we finish this lesson there may be no field trip to the aquarium."

Suddenly this overly bubbly child instantaneously appears motionless with a blank stare reminiscent of the "1000-yard stare" seen in combat soldiers returning from a fierce battle. It lasts only seconds but all of a sudden Timmy's mood has transformed from excited to anxious. All attempts to calm him down seem to fail as he perseverates now on the possibility of not going despite reassurances that he will go. All he heard was that there may be no field trip, which created a freeze response that prevented him from hearing anything else, including reassurances.

If ever while working with an individual, especially a young child, they just burst into tears while you are talking with them chances are something you said surprised them enough to trigger a freeze and then an anxiety response. The freeze response always occurs before a fight or flight response. It is critical that you learn to identify how the individual you are working with manifests this response because it will also not only help to minimize potential meltdowns but will be a key element in determining if the individual is spiraling into meltdown or just using manipulative behavior in the form of a tantrum.

MY PERSONAL EXPERIENCE WITH THE FREEZE RESPONSE

This has happened to me even as an adult. Back in 2005 I decided to have myself tested through a neuro-psychological evaluation because I knew I was different from everyone else and I wanted to know why I had such communication difficulties in social settings and why I had these near hysterical episodes when things didn't go as planned. This testing process consisted of an 8–10 hour battery of tests to see how the brain processes information. In many of the subtests it required the tester to ask questions that were poorly defined and vague. As an adult with a master's degree I felt confident that I could ask for clarity so I could answer the question succinctly. The first time I told her I didn't understand the question and could she be more specific she replied that she couldn't as it would "pollute" the validity of the test. Immediately my mouth dropped, I became speechless; despite her trying to say something else I didn't hear anything. My blank stare registered no visual input. I was literally "frozen" for a millisecond. I was taken by complete surprise at her "no" response. My brain became totally focused on the "no" and couldn't move on. I didn't understand how clarifying a vague question would ruin the test. I had a history of always asking for clarification when talking with people who then rephrased things so I understood. Immediately I began to spiral downward in a wave of anxiety of not being able to answer the questions appropriately and thereby not conveying how intelligent I was and scoring overall at a subpar level.

The tester tried to verbally reassure me but my fight response was triggered so all I was capable of doing was crying and verbally (in rather strong language) tearing apart the entire design and testing procedures of this evaluation. Thankfully she knew I was autistic before I did and didn't see this flagrant outburst of emotion as a tantrum but an unintentional response of frustration and bewilderment. Knowing I was in a meltdown of sorts she just allowed me to vent without herself becoming confrontational until I expended all my energy (adrenaline rush). It was pointless to even attempt to interact logically with me at that time as I was cognitively unable to process any information. Once I calmed down I was horrified by my behavior and apologized profusely and then was able to accept her reassurances that I wasn't tantruming but having a meltdown. Once calm I was able to listen to her explanation of why she wasn't allowed to clarify questions and although I didn't like it I now understood why and it didn't come as a surprise when it happened again numerous times throughout the testing procedure.

As you can see anxiety and the freeze–fight–flight response are intimately connected. It is the explanation for some of our behaviors but not all. In this chapter I have covered the instinctual responses to anxiety but there is also anxiety that isn't directly connected to this response that seems to govern our reasoning capability and negatively affect our overall ability to just "enjoy the moment" without worry. This sense of worry is a dominant characteristic that seems to govern every aspect of our daily life. I will give you a much better understanding of what we are thinking and feeling and why we appear to live in a constant of worry in the next chapter.

CHAPTER 3

How Anxiety Impacts Our Cognitive Abilities

In the last chapter I talked about how the freeze, fight, and flight response is an instinctual non cognitive reaction to being taken by surprise. The near constant state of hypervigilance which in many cases manifests itself through heightened senses creates a natural level of anxiety as a primal means of self preservation. What about anxiety not directly related to this response? What about the person with autism who seems to constantly worry or "obsess" over highly unlikely scenarios even when things are going according to plan or script? Why can't we just stop worrying about the unknown and at least "enjoy the moment"? Why do some children, when anxious, seem to badger us with questions they already know the answer to?

Back in Chapter 1 I discussed how important it is not only to have a script but to stay on script every waking moment. So important is this concept to us that any deviation creates great angst. Living in a society that blatantly engages in deceitful practices creates chaos within the autistic individual because reality is unclear. What is said may not be what is done, which translates into unpredictability, which is a concept we cannot embrace. We crave structure and order, following through with what is said, and sticking to the predetermined timetable for the day. The society I live in goes contrary to this concept. Being autistic and trying to navigate something as simple as grocery shopping can be stressful and anxiety provoking in a world that isn't autistic friendly.

The stress of navigating through the simple task of shopping

Just today I went shopping for groceries at our local food store. Being highly attuned to details, I had noticed this past winter that every other week when I went in to purchase food, prices jumped by a minimum of 25 cents. For the last three consecutive weeks this summer prices did not increase and some items actually saw a reduction in price. Naturally suspicious, I quickly noticed what many other consumers hadn't yet: the containers contained one third less product. I saw that the price of a container of ice cream was still $2.50 but when I picked up a container, instead of being a half gallon, which it has been for decades, it is now one and a half. quarts. Coffee cans that used to weigh one pound have dropped to 11 ounces yet the cans are still the same size. In the detergent aisle I noticed bottles of liquid soap that had printed on the front label in bold highlights, "New and Improved," by proclaiming a redesign of the bottle to ensure easier gripping. Right under the product there was a price reduction tag stating that their product was consumer friendly because it cost less than its competitors. Thinking this sounded too good to be true, I reached behind the row of bottles to find a bottle left over from previous shipments. This bottle contained six ounces more than the "New and Improved" bottles, and was just as easy to grip with one hand. I can't help but marvel at how many companies use blatant deception to market their product and wonder why consumers just accept this as inevitable and don't get irate at such practices. Feeling outraged whenever I discover such a marketing scheme I always point it out to any nearby shoppers strolling down my aisle. They acknowledge it isn't fair but overall the responses I get from them revolve around just accepting what is because you can't change it. Of course I want to explain the concept of a boycott but I restrain myself from doing so in fear of being viewed as a revolutionary or anti-establishment trouble maker.

If that isn't bad enough I head to the check-out lane to pay for my items. I have only four items in my hand basket so I proceed to the "express check-out lane." I don't know how it is in other countries but here in the United States most grocery stores have an express lane designed for the convenience of the shopper with fewer than ten items so that they don't have to wait in long lines behind shopping carts overflowing with groceries. I am number nine in line for the register and it seems to be moving slower than the regular lanes. I can't help, while I am waiting impatiently, counting the number of items each person has in front of me. Six of them have items totaling anywhere from 19 to 23. A large placard beside this lane says ten items or fewer while overhead the register light also has the ten items rule clearly marked so that there is no confusion. This creates some anxiety within me because here you have a "rule" to be followed, yet some selfish shoppers just disregard it without any consequence, so how am I to judge what societal rules are to be followed? What is the rationale behind creating a universal rule that won't be universally followed? Who decides which person will be held accountable for violation of that rule? The outright refusal of these six consumers to honor this rule means I am subjected to a longer wait time with longer exposure to sensory issues that can build up until it finally becomes a sensory overload meltdown. When finally it is my turn to be rung up, the cashier lady asks a question to which she doesn't want a truthful answer. I in turn am not only expected to give a lie in response but feign interest in her personal well being.

She begins with, "Hi, and how are you today?"

The universal response that is expected is, "I am fine, thank you, and how are you?"

Why this charade of pretending to be interested in our well being? I have been known on occasion to respond truthfully and convey that I wasn't well and list the reasons why. Every time I do that the sales people seem completely shocked and unable to respond. They were the ones who initiated the question of the status of my well being for that day. Why must I lie just because society expects me to? That is anxiety provoking in itself. If you are not truly interested in someone else's well being wouldn't it make more logical sense to just not ask how they are doing in the first place? Why not just exchange facts instead? It would be refreshing if the "conversation" started off, while she was scanning my box of herbal green tea, with my sharing of the fact that Chinese researchers have found that people who drink two cups of green tea daily had DNA that looked younger than those who didn't drink green tea.

As I walk out into the parking lot I notice a large banner draped across the front entrance of the hardware store across the parking lot. It reads, "50–75% off in stock items sale." Naturally curious I walk over to explore bargains I cannot refuse, which I hadn't planned to do, therefore I have deviated from the set timeframe I scripted for going shopping. As I enter, much to my dismay I see that this "sale" is limited to "selected items only," comprising one aisle of discontinued or returned merchandise. Drawing in potential customers by such deliberately misleading means doesn't make any sense. The theory is that once you draw a person in, chances are they will decide since they are there anyway to look around and perhaps buy something else. This was a waste of time which set me behind my schedule and script.

People with autism see the world in black and white, there are no shades of gray. Going off script to check out the hardware store may only have cost five minutes extra time, which to non autistic people seems insignificant, but to an autistic person five minutes is a complete break in the predetermined schedule set in our minds. It isn't about "degrees" of being off script; going off script for any length of time is a complete break and results in a feeling of anxiety. Why? It is because we thrive on scripts, which seem to create a sense of order, structure, and predictability in a world that is so unpredictable. Unpredictability is our number one enemy, which we fear beyond measure. I know that I can't force the world to adapt to my scripts. I am merely pointing out our inherent weakness of not being tolerant towards spontaneity, not staying on script, and the unpredictability of human nature. Even a five-minute deviation off script will give birth to anxiety about the remaining timeframe in this set script. I have timed this food shopping excursion so that I am away from the shopping center ten minutes before the nearby school lets the children out for the day. What if the school's clock is five minutes faster than my watch and lets out five minutes early? My five-minute delay means now I may run the risk of being caught behind school buses dropping off children at every corner, throwing me even further off my timetable and my next appointment at the doctor's office.

Going off script even slightly can easily lead to the domino effect where everything else that occurs after this deviation is no longer predictable. For that reason alone I become anxious, needing to make a hasty exit from the hardware store to make up the lost time so that I don't run into the potential school bus issue. Being so overly focused on repairing this script I scurry to my vehicle not registering anything but staying on script. I have on occasion not noticed or acknowledged someone who knew me calling out hello as I hurried past them in an attempt to regain my original pre-determined schedule. I came across as rude or intentionally ignoring people who took it personally because their feelings got hurt by my lack of acknowledgement. Honestly, it wasn't a deliberate act on my part. My problem solving skill at that moment was to get back on my timeframe by physically increasing my walking pace, thereby gaining valuable seconds towards making up the lost five minutes, and missing being stuck behind the school buses. Although I was visibly anxious to others, I didn't acknowledge or "feel" that emotion because I was too overly focused on problem solving which was more important.

From the hardware store I drive to a doctor's appointment set for 1:00 pm. I arrive at 12:50 pm. Upon entering the office the receptionist states, "The doctor will be with you shortly."

I am led into his office 55 minutes after my designated appointment time. Isn't it funny how despite having an appointment time we are resigned to waiting well past that time without complaint, yet if I am so much as ten minutes late the receptionist gives my appointment away to the next in line. Again waiting in the reception area for an undisclosed time is unscripted time and very unpredictable. Magazines on the coffee table or stand designed to alleviate the boredom while you wait are hard to pick up and read because, without knowing exactly when you will be seen, how can you know if you will be able to finish reading some interesting article before being asked to follow the nurse or receptionist into the doctor's office? I will discuss transitions and anxiety in detail later in this book but suffice it to say here that autistic people are hard pressed to just drop some unfinished business and move on to something else. If by chance I do find something worth reading while I am waiting I cannot just put down the magazine, get up, and follow the receptionist or nurse into the doctor's office. It usually goes one of two ways: either I take the magazine with me into the office and must finish reading it before I can engage in any conversation, or I do not get up until I have finished the article. Since both are socially deemed inappropriate I avoid this dilemma by not looking at the magazine selection in the first place.

On the way home from the doctor's office I listen to the news on public radio. The entire broadcast is dominated by the continuing oil spill in the Gulf of Mexico. Accusations of how the oil company deliberately misled the government and its people by reporting a much lesser amount of oil gushing from the ocean floor, as well as serious disregard for safety protocols that led to the disaster, become very disheartening. The magnitude of the consequences can't be measured and it may take decades to fully understand the environmental impact. I begin to feel anxious as the news continues on about how seafood prices are expected to soar in the coming months due to the widespread contamination of oil and the speculation of disastrous long term environmental impacts. My anxiety focuses the on volatility and unpredictability of the commodities market. Will gasoline prices rise astronomically in the coming months causing dramatic price increases in everything we purchase from food to household necessities? How can I better brace myself for the impact it will have on my budget? Should I stock up on certain items now before prices soar? Why was there a failure to notice the warning signs on the rig or follow safety procedures that could have averted this disaster?

People with high functioning forms of autism will naturally try to come up with another back up script whenever they feel threatened by a break in the continuity of how they perceived their own personal future would unfold, even for events such as the oil spill which carries such a magnitude of uncertainties that it is impossible to come up with a contingency for every possibility. Remember it's not necessarily about finding a contingency plan for every potential scenario that relieves anxiety, but rather gaining a sense of control again by creating a logical plan, even if only theoretical, which reduces our anxiety in that situation. It all comes back to our being unable to handle unpredictability and having scripts go awry.

A sense of relief sets in as I finally arrive home. As I begin unpacking my shopping bags someone knocks on the front door. I answer it only to find two missionaries asking if I know the world is going to end soon. They tell me they have hard evidence of this coming calamity. Intrigued, I invite them in to hear what facts they have as evidence of the world's apparent demise. Instead I get badgered about how I will be in eternal agony writhing in a sea of flames if I don't repent and accept Jesus as my personal savior. I demand evidence of such torture and instead they recite verbatim selected passages taken out of context from a manuscript written almost two thousand years ago and accepted as truth by much of the world, based on faith. Upset by this intrusion I demand that they leave. I decide to calm down by going online and checking my emails. In my account I notice an unread email from my girlfriend. The title, in bold capital letters reads, "URGENT, PLEASE READ, I NEED YOUR HELP." This sounds serious. I immediately open the email in which she explains to me she has just had her wallet stolen with all her money from the hotel she is staying at in Nigeria. She asks me to wire her one thousand U.S. dollars so that she can return home. I ponder how this can be, as I just saw her today at the grocery store while I was shopping. No doubt one of many internet fraud scams. Even in the privacy of my own home I am not safe from the dishonesty of the outside world.

I am anxious because I question why such internet practices such as scamming, phishing, or worms and viruses don't result in a massive public prosecution of such crimes. I can't help but feel anxiety every time I turn on my computer worrying about these scammers infiltrating my personal computer or accessing my personal information from my bank or town records. Why are there only public announcements and news bulletins that warn us of the latest scam? Why must I go out and keep purchasing the latest computer virus protection that quickly becomes outdated as hackers work on overriding those safeguards? I have a laptop that is so old that it doesn't have the Microsoft Word program. This manuscript had to be submitted in Word so I went out and bought a brand new laptop with Word capability. The sales associate who sold me the computer put the fear of God into me by explaining the countless ways my computer can be "corrupted" or compromised by hackers and spies despite the latest anti-spyware and virus protection. It would make more logical sense to devote time and energy to punishing cyber crimes, no matter what their country of origin, so that this type of crime isn't so lucrative. Without any guarantee that I can keep my expensive computer safe naturally I am anxious every time I go online. I have dealt with this anxiety by using my new computer solely for the purpose of writing this book. No internet connection means I don't have to worry about what could cause a computer crash resulting in months of hard work lost. Instead I go online with my ten-year-old laptop. It is so old its systems are failing but it still works for emails and for looking things up on the internet. There is no personal information stored in there so if something or someone were to corrupt and/or crash that old computer it wouldn't be a personal tragedy.

Societal inconsistencies

In a typical day most non autistic people wouldn't even notice the inconsistencies and misrepresentations of the truth in my previous shopping excursion example, or would not be too adversely affected by it because they have infiltrated daily activities. Truth in many areas that was once concrete has now become open to personal interpretation; a "white lie." By definition a lie is a deliberate misrepresentation of a truthful fact. In Exodus, the Ten Commandments states that lying is a sin: "thou shalt not bear false witness [lie] against thy neighbor" (King James Version). A white lie is a "bending" of the truth for many reasons, but as long as it doesn't seriously harm another is considered an acceptable practice. In truth it is an oxymoron because adding the word "white" which denotes purity, to the word "lie" which denotes deception, cancels each other out.

Even laws designed to protect citizens from terrorism can seem irrational and anxiety provoking to an autistic person like me. In the state of Maine it is legal to have ammunition for firearms shipped or mailed to your residence. Yesterday I called a farm supply company to order a brand new 15 gallon portable plastic gasoline container for my garden tractor. I was informed that I could not purchase this item because in the state of Maine it is illegal to ship empty gasoline containers through the mail because they could be used in the manufacture of bombs. I have found it is useless to question this logic because the fear of terrorism is so rampant that it can border on paranoia. I ended up shipping this harmless empty new container to my mother and her husband's home in Massachusetts. In their state it is illegal to have any firearm parts or ammunition delivered to a residence but it is legal to ship empty new gasoline containers. It is an easy drive between Maine and Massachusetts so if a terrorist really needed a gas can and ammunition it would be no real effort. I don't feel I can sleep any better at night knowing these laws will make it harder for terrorist cells to strike here in small town America. My anxiety stems mainly from not understanding the logic of it. I can't get clear answers as to why these laws are deemed as valuable in protecting citizens. Many of them are based on rhetoric and aren't even enforceable. Some laws were enacted just to make the public "feel good" that homeland security is strong. For an autistic person it is very difficult to blindly accept any rule or law when there is no justification for it, especially when we see areas where failure is likely.

When I first began flying to my seminar destinations I was very careful about what was allowed through security screening and I made sure I was compliant. On one of my trips to the south I had the chance to visit Civil War battlefields and I had permission from a landowner to do a little digging for artifacts near one of the battlefields. I found the bottom part of a wine bottle along with other shards of bottle glass and rusted jagged metal sword scabbards. While there I took four ordinary rocks the size of golf balls for my geological collection. In the airport on my way home I was flagged going through the screening process for suspicious items. After tearing apart my carry on bag I was told by airport authorities that my rocks could be used as a dangerous weapon and would have to be confiscated. What didn't make any sense was the fact that they allowed me in my carry on bag to bring on the plane the extremely sharp large pieces of broken glass and rusted metal. In theory I find razor sharp objects much more dangerous than an egg-sized rounded rock. Metal nail files aren't allowed in a carry on because they could be sharpened and used as a knife. What is the point of confiscating potential weapons such as pocket-sized folding scissors, or tweezers, or a four-ounce tube of toothpaste, yet allowing broken glass to be carried on? It is inconsistencies like these that permeate just about every area of our lives. As a person with autism daily life is naturally anxiety provoking because in our quest for concrete answers and logic it is maddening trying to understand the everyday inconsistencies of societal customs and laws. Our frustration over such discrepancies is equal to the intensity of the frustration a non autistic person would feel over some social injustice, such as domestic violence or child pornography.

A world of absolutes: a major reason for anxiety

Here is a major reason why individuals with autism appear to be in a near constant state of anxiety. Autistic individuals live in a world of absolutes. For every question there must be a logical or black and white answer. Randomness doesn't exist in our minds. There is a reason for everything and everything has a reason. We are by nature compelled to seek a logical answer to any question or problem throughout our lives. Obviously, in a world that lives contrary to our needs, anxiety is related to not understanding the rationale behind something or not getting a definitive answer to a question. Our overly developed logical brain dominates our every thought. It is said that autistic people are emotionally detached or lack the awareness of "feelings" in themselves or in others. We often come across as cold and callous to the emotional needs of other people. It is not because we lack the ability to feel emotion. We do feel all sorts of emotions, just like anyone else, but because we are driven to find an answer, expressing our feelings is irrelevant as it won't aid in finding a resolution to the problem at hand. So while we are feeling upset or sad on the inside, it may not be verbally expressed because our mind is too busy trying to process a logical solution which takes precedence over emotion. This is a key point in understanding why autistic individuals when anxious tend to "obsess" or "perseverate" on the problem or issue at hand, despite reassurances from those around them to not worry as it will work out.

Asking how or what we are feeling when distressed usually results in non ability to respond to that query, further intense perseveration, wanting to be left alone, and generally a marked increase in anxiety. When non autistic individuals get anxious or have a bad day they tend to "vent" how they feel to a friend, or perhaps seek the counseling services of a therapist to explore what they feel. Current psychotherapy is designed to analyze how and what a person feels and teach them the tools needed to not only feel better about themselves but also to help them to find the answer on their own. I know this because I have a master's degree in Counseling. I remember my classroom role playing sessions designed to teach us clinical listening skills. It used to frustrate me no end to just sit and listen intently to my "client" go on and on expressing their feelings about the issue at hand with me having to interject every now and then, "And how does that make you feel?" That just encouraged them to "open up" and continue expressing how they felt. I wanted so badly to interrupt and tell them to stop harping on what they were feeling and start problem solving, which would remedy how they felt much faster than wasting a full hour on describing what they feel. I had already got the gist of that after the first ten minutes of the session. I am positive therapists all over the world breathed a sigh of relief when I decided that traditional counseling wasn't going to be my forte. I went on to become a crisis counselor at a homeless shelter where I dealt with finding practical solutions for immediate problems centered on basic needs such as food, shelter, clothing, and money. These clients used to come to me very anxious and upset and would leave feeling much better because I was able with my creative thinking style to come up with some non traditional means of solving their dilemma.

What are we "feeling"?

Individuals like me with autism when we get anxious or upset don't have an interest in what we are feeling. We want a concrete answer, a fix for the problem, or for things to go back to the way they were. We tend to withdraw from people because under stress the last thing we need is the added burden of trying to get the non autistic person to understand that our anxiety, about something outwardly trivial to anyone but us, is a catastrophic ordeal. A group therapy session where an autistic individual is among non autistic participants is of little value because we generally don't care what others are thinking or feeling when all our internal voice keeps shouting in our head screaming for us to "FIX THIS PROBLEM NOW!" We become disinterested in the group as a whole, internally distracted by our own immediate issue at hand and we appear uncooperative to the rest of the group. Individual therapy sessions using traditional interventions geared towards exploring feelings are also counterproductive in lessening our anxiety levels for the same reason.

Let me illustrate this with the following scenario. I will give you a situation and then two approaches of dealing with this same problem. The first will be the viewpoint from a non autistic person seeking counseling and the second from an autistic perspective on the same problem. I am able to describe the non autistic approach because I polled many people asking them how they would handle the following situation. All of them gave very similar responses to my example.

Let's assume that you are washing the family laundry. As you toss your spouse's shirt into the washing machine you notice there is a folded piece of paper in the breast pocket. Naturally you decide to remove it before washing. This note has a rather fragrant odor to it so for curiosity's sake you open and read the note. Much to your horror the note is an intimate explicit love letter written to your spouse by someone other than you. What would you be thinking or feeling at that moment?

Consumed in disbelief you anxiously await your spouse's return home from work four hours later. You are unable to even perform the daily mundane chores you normally do during this period so you sit on the couch and do nothing out of utter disbelief. What would your thoughts be dominated by during that four-hour timeframe?

Immediately they enter the house you confront them, demanding an explanation. They confess to you that your worst fears of infidelity are true. They are in love with another person. You are so emotionally devastated you call your best friend to tell your tale of betrayal. They offer you affirmation and validation that you are a victim of such a wretched betrayal and suggest that you see a therapist to help you to cope with this emotionally crushing situation. You make an appointment to see a psychotherapist. At the start of the session you are wringing your hands constantly, seem easily distracted, and unable to concentrate long enough to fill out the written patient questionnaire. The therapist notices your anxiety and states the obvious, "You appear anxious today, how can I help you?"

With that you begin to explain why you are there but the emotions of being so hurt come out and you can't stop sobbing. You explain that you just found out about your spouse's multiple infidelities and you don't know what to do. You question your own self worth. You wonder how this could have happened and why your spouse would do something so hurtful.

Most likely the therapist would reassure you that you are not a bad person, explain that it is natural for you to feel all sorts of emotions from rage to despair, affirm to you that this is a terrible thing to happen to anyone and that they will be there to listen and work through all those rejection, despair, and abandonment emotions with you. Their goal is to return you to a somewhat normal emotional state of well being.

Now let's approach this exact same issue from the autistic perspective.

While doing the laundry I notice a piece of paper in my husband's shirt pocket. I remove it, read it, and discover he is having an affair. My first thoughts are not about betrayal but about how this revelation will take away all that I have become accustomed to in terms of predictability and routine in my marriage and household. My second thought focuses solely on how to protect myself from the ramifications of his adultery. I have four hours until my husband returns from work. I concentrate on finishing all planned chores quickly so I can then concentrate on this dilemma. I finish within two hours so I systematically go through our finances, emails, and phone records looking for evidence to confirm his indiscretion and check the overall status of our finances so I can assess how I will manage financially should we divorce. When he comes home I confront him and he confesses. I become very angry over the fact that now things will change forever destroying the comfortable routine I had become accustomed to. I call a friend asking what forms of punitive measures I should employ against him which would be appropriate for this situation. After systematically explaining that all vengeful methods I was considering would fail, she tells me that I should see a therapist for help. I take her advice and make an appointment.

At the start of the session my anxiety was clearly evident by the constant rocking, repetitive hand gestures, and my being easily startled by even the slightest noises or distractions. When the therapist asks why I have come to see him I give the exact same reason, "I just found out my husband has been having multiple affairs and I don't know what to do."

The therapist tries to reassure me that I am not a bad person but I interrupt him saying I already know that because it wasn't I but my husband who had the affair so therefore he is the bad person.

I become more visibly upset and tell him that I came to him for help. My interruption has caught him off guard and in an attempt to defuse my anxiety he asks what I am feeling at that moment. This only increases my frustration and I respond with, "I don't care how I feel right now as it doesn't matter. I am obviously miserable, who wouldn't be? He ruined my life and I need definite answers on what to do."

The key here is in understanding what I was expressing as my concern in the last sentence. "He ruined my life" didn't refer to my being unable to ever trust again but a loss of predictability in my living arrangement. Needing definite answers referred to an action plan of what steps I should take next to regain a sense of order and predictability for future living arrangements.

I came to the therapist to seek tangible answers because with my lack of executive functioning skills and impulsiveness I was unable to come up with working solutions to restore my world of predictability. My need to find an answer to this problem as it directly related to my future physical well being was so paramount I could not process what I was feeling emotionally, despite outward signs of anxiety.

In this hypothetical situation what should the therapist do? Most autistic individuals will want help in finding practical solutions. In this case the therapist could list the logical rational options available to me: "Well, Deb, these are your options. Number one you can leave him and get a divorce. Number two you can forgive him and forget it ever happened. Number three you can attempt to seek marriage counseling with him."

Then the therapist would list the pros and cons for each option and then say that's it for options. I must choose one after careful deliberation, so I should go home and think about it until the next session. He then sets up an action plan to help in planning what actions my choice will require me to take. Before the end of the session I appear calmer and not so excitable. I apologize for my behavior, noting I was initially so anxious over not having a tangible plan that I had a hard time controlling my outbursts. Once I am comfortable with knowing I have "script" options I am able to finally discuss how betrayal of trust doesn't feel good emotionally.

Problem solving from the autistic viewpoint

Remember when an autistic person goes off any script the immediate need is not an emotional one but a practical one, with solutions or a "back up" plan. So overpowering is this need to find a solution it doesn't allow for self awareness of emotions we are experiencing at that moment. No matter how visibly distressed, upset, or anxious the person may be, your focusing on what they are feeling will not de-escalate the situation. They are in need of a solution before anything else can be dealt with. Your best strategy for dealing with this type of anxiety is to look at the logical options available and offer a working plan. To calm an autistic individual down it is imperative that you offer logical solutions in very concrete language during this phase. Avoid using phrases designed to offer reassurances such as, "Don't worry things will work out eventually."

While this may offer hope to a non autistic person, to an autistic person it is seen as an act of rejection because offering vague reassurances means that our problem is seen as an overreaction and not worthy of finding a solution. It adds to our frustration level because our problem isn't taken seriously. I know that isn't the intent of a well meaning intervener but that is how it is perceived at that moment because even the minutest problem can be monumental to us not because of the severity of the issue but because our script didn't follow the sequence it was supposed to.

The fear of unpredictability

I can't emphasize enough how critical it is for you, the reader, to understand that staying on any script, whether simple or complicated, is the sole means of keeping anxiety at a minimum. Even the smallest breach, no matter how insignificant it may seem, becomes a crisis to us because all we register at that moment is unpredictability. We fear unpredictability above all else because we are out of control of our environment. We are unable to process anything anyone says unless it involves a practical immediate solution. People have strong opinions regarding just how much an autistic individual must learn to "accept" the unpredictability of life and the fact that the world cannot revolve around their personal scripts. It is not my intent to create controversy over this heated issue by advocating rigid adherence to any script so as to keep the autistic individual calm. I am merely pointing out why we get so anxious when events don't follow a predetermined order. It is part of our neurological makeup that can't be permanently extinguished. As adults with autism we will continually have to find compromises and creative solutions to deal with the unpredictability of life. No one ever said that having autism would be easy. My insatiable need for scripting everything from making breakfast to going away on a speaking tour takes considerable time, effort, and planning, with constant contingencies built in as a safeguard. I am sure life would be less complicated if I didn't have to engage in this constant need for order but I have come to accept that I cannot change my neurological makeup. I will never out of free will embrace spontaneity or enjoy variety as the spice of life. Instead of focusing my energies on what I cannot change I try to create personal daily scripts that offer a low impact, least disruptive effect on individuals I encounter.

Sometimes it means I must keep my social interactions to a bare minimum in order to keep to my rigid adherence of a script. I much prefer to be alone and calm than completely stressed out in front of others because they didn't stick to the plan. As I mentioned in Chapter 1, it is not uncommon for me and my husband to take separate vehicles when going to a social function or even shopping. My husband generally fails to be ready to leave on time. This creates rising anxiety because the continuity of my timeframe has been broken. Before I was diagnosed and understood autism these episodes would result in heated arguments where my husband always accused me of being intolerant of minor time delays. Now we agree to a certain arrival time for attending a planned social function and we take separate vehicles. This way I get to arrive and leave according to my script and my husband's tardiness won't alter my very punctual arrival and departure times. My script for arriving is a solo script, meaning that if my husband shows up "fashionably late" it doesn't negatively impact me because he was not factored into my arrival plans and therefore not required to adhere to that script. Arriving separately but calm is a much better alternative than arriving as couple who have argued all the way there.

Stimming
STIMMING DEFUSES RISING ANXIETY LEVELS

One major way we defuse increasing anxiety is through self stimming. Self stimming is a very important coping mechanism autistic individuals engage in to calm themselves down during periods of increasing anxiety. Self stim behaviors include (but aren't limited to) the following: hand flapping, rocking, shaking a leg, finger flicking, humming, nervous twitches or tics, singing or repeating the same song or phrases over and over again, audible noises, vigorous hand rubbing, or drizzling water or sand in front of their faces with their fingers. Every human being stims at certain stressful points in their life but autistic individuals do it with much more intensity and frequency as it is our number one coping mechanism for handling anxiety. Anxiety increases the level of adrenaline that flows through our body preparing us for a fight or flight response. Engaging in some sort of repetitive physical task helps to burn off some of this rising adrenaline so that we don't explode (figuratively). Consider it a relief valve of sorts. It is a natural coping mechanism employed by all human beings. If you have ever witnessed a confrontation between two people you have noticed how adrenaline levels build rather quickly in this instinctual fight response. The argument visibly escalates. When others are present someone may intervene to de-escalate the situation by asking one person to take a walk to cool off. The act of walking helps decrease the physical levels of adrenaline coursing through the veins, calming the individual down. Notice during escalating arguments that reason and logic give way to irrational accusations and incorrect facts. What is happening is that as the adrenaline increases the anxiety increases, pushing the brain closer to a full non cognitive instinctual preservation state designed to react and not think—the fight or flight response. It does no good to try to reason with a person in such a state because their processing and reasoning abilities are temporarily not functioning and well meaning attempts will be perceived as hostile by them. If someone can manage to get the person to take a walk they generally return in a somewhat calmer state.

Walking is a method of stimming. We would never deny an angry person in such a confrontation the opportunity to take a walk to defuse. At that moment their anxiety level is so heightened it is nearly impossible for them to come up with rational calm solutions to the confrontation. It is the same concept in individuals with autism. When their anxiety level is rising so is their adrenaline. As adrenaline rises cognitive processing and thinking decreases. Repetitive engagement in some physical motion will burn up some of the adrenaline, thereby reducing the anxiety level somewhat. It is critical that the child or adult be allowed to stim in some form at this time as it is a natural coping mechanism. That being said, I am aware that many school districts view stimming as disruptive to the other students in the classroom. If a less disruptive form of stimming isn't available, the best solution is to allow the child time to stim in whatever manner calms them down away from the class, in a private partitioned off area at the back of the class, for instance. In college when I became particularly stressed during a lecture I would just excuse myself and go to the women's washroom. I would then go into an empty stall, shut the door, and spend a few minutes just flapping my hands to calm down. No one could see me so it couldn't be viewed as disruptive to my classmates and at the same time allowed me the freedom to self regulate my anxiety level in a manner that I knew would be successful. I still employ that very technique today. People with autism need a physical release. Attempting to discuss how they are feeling at that moment or asking them to calm down will be met with agitated responses at first graduating to aggressive responses if they are denied a physical form of de-stressing through stimming.

I strongly urge autistic readers to contact an occupational therapist and discuss stimming issues with them. They are experts in this field and can help find appropriate stimming responses for anxiety, the best stim tools to fit an individual's needs. No two individuals are alike in regards to stimming preferences so don't mistakenly assume what works for one child or adult will automatically work for another. It could actually escalate the situation. This is particularly true in settings with multiple individuals with autism. Society, I believe, is too focused on managing the symptoms rather than the underlying causes of any problem. So much energy goes into palliative measures to eliminate symptoms without exploring how to correct the underlying cause. Most of my school consultations are for disruptive stim behavior in the classroom. On numerous occasions my directions were to "make the behavior stop." When I observe intense stimming my first goal is to find the underlying cause, why the child is stimming, as opposed to immediately working on a behavioral plan to change the form of stimming. Stimming is a reaction to something. I try to rule out all plausible underlying causes such as schedule changes, sensory issues, communication difficulties, etc., before focusing on the stim behavior. Correcting an underlying issue may be the fastest way to stop the stimming behavior, and being autistic gives me the distinct advantage of being able to experience the environment from the child's autistic vantage point. I am much more sensitive to minor fluctuations in a surrounding environment than a non autistic person.

I should point out that good anxiety as well as bad anxiety will elicit intense stimming as the anxiety level increases. Sometimes children and adults can get so excited anticipating a favorite outing or activity that it increases their adrenaline levels just as much as for bad anxiety. In these cases they stim for the same physiological but different emotional reasons. This is true of any child. I have been witness to countless non autistic children "jumping for joy" over receiving a highly anticipated birthday gift or Christmas present. It is natural and normal and an autistic child is no different in those situations. Sometimes well meaning adults tend to micro-manage an autistic child's every behavior, forgetting that the autistic child is still just a child and will engage in good and bad behavior typical of the stage of childhood development they are in.

STIMMING DONE SOLELY OUT OF HABIT

Sometimes an individual will engage in continuous stimming even when not anxious. That stimming is usually related to habit, not getting a sensory need met, or is engaged in out of plain boredom. There are rare occasions where an individual who is physically hurt or not feeling well will engage in constant stimming without any apparent obvious reason to those around them. Stimming, as with any other type of behavior, is always a form of communication. Always rule out any potential underlying cause for the stimming before attributing it to disruptive behavior. The intensity of the stimming will also give you a clue to how high the anxiety level is. Generally speaking the stimming intensity will increase with increases in the anxiety level. Don't assume minor stimming means that the individual is able to totally self regulate their anxiety levels at all times. In most cases stimming of any sort is a reaction. Be vigilant in observing whether the stimming maintains its current level or begins to increase. Look for signs that the stimming is a response to increasing anxiety levels. The classic example I see is of the individual who begins to get nervous during an activity and begins to flap their hands down by their sides. If the underlying problem isn't addressed I notice the hands and the flapping motion rising from their sides up to hip level. As the anxiety level rises so do their hands and when I see the flapping of hands at chest height I know they are about to have a meltdown. Stimming and its intensity is a perfect sign to look for if you are worried about a pending meltdown. Know your client's behavioral patterns and how they express frustration and be aware of those sometimes subtle "signs" and don't ignore them. Remember for us autistics our anxiety level is directly correlated to the problem. Problem solve first as that is the number one calming strategy. Sometimes the solution is a simple one, such as clarifying a miscommunication, removing a sensory trigger, or clarifying a question or command.

The child who keeps badgering you with questions they already know the answer to

There are many reasons for such behavior and it is difficult to give you just one cause that would apply in all situations. Sometimes it is done to annoy or as a game, but it can also be a common nervous response. I have witnessed this behavior in quite a few autistic children when uncertainty was the underlying cause. I saw it as a plea for affirmation that events would stay on script.

In one case I was spending the night with a friend who had two children, one of whom had Asperger's Syndrome. We had all planned to go out for ice cream at four o'clock in the afternoon. The non autistic child was misbehaving so the mother, addressing only him, said, "If you keep behaving badly there will be no ice cream for you this afternoon."

The Asperger's child overheard this conversation and immediately began to fidget and continuously ask his mother what time we would be going for an ice cream and before she could answer he would state the correct time. After about the fifth time she looked at me, bewildered, complaining that now her autistic son decided to join his brother in misbehaving as a means of gaining her attention. To me it was clear that her autistic son wasn't misbehaving but becoming anxious. His anxiety stemmed from her reprimanding her other son by threatening "no ice cream." When the little boy turned to me and began asking and answering the same question over and over again I interrupted him. I asked him to wait quietly while I asked his mother to clarify if we were still going for an ice cream. At first the mother was almost distraught, thinking this question and answer "game" was contagious, as now I was asking what time we were going for ice cream. I phrased my question a little differently knowing the autistic child was listening intently to what I was asking. I asked, "I am wondering if we are still planning on going for our ice cream at four o'clock this afternoon. The reason I am wondering is because in your reprimand to your older non autistic child you threatened he would not get an ice cream if he misbehaved. Knowing that you have no baby sitter to watch him and you don't leave your children unattended, if he continues to misbehave how will his punishment affect us? Will we still be able to go to get an ice cream, which is a treat I am looking forward to?"

She quickly responded, saying it was never her intent to cancel the outing, but to have her son if he continued to misbehave come along but not receive an ice cream. Although I felt the punishment of having a child having to watch us eat ice cream and not get one if he kept misbehaving was rather unkind, it was not my place to question a mother's disciplinary actions, especially when I have no children of my own. As soon as she responded by clarifying her intent the Asperger's son ceased badgering us with the question he already knew the answer to. I pointed out that her reprimand, while clear to her older son, was vague and not concrete enough for her autistic child. He immediately began logically processing how his mother's reprimand towards his older brother would affect the plan or script of going out for ice cream. He read unpredictability and going off script in her reprimand and began looking for affirmation that the script of this outing would not be canceled due to something out of his control. In this case he felt threatened by an indirect reprimand as it related to an anticipated event he was eagerly looking to. The uncertainty was enough to raise his anxiety level to the point where he couldn't focus on anything else until he had affirmation that plans had not changed.

Should we use medication to help reduce anxiety levels in individuals with autism?

It is one of the frequently asked questions wherever I speak. There should never be a "blanket answer" of yes or no to this question. It must be reviewed on an individual basis, taking into account other contributing factors and conditions, physical and mental. I will say I have strong personal feelings against arbitrarily medicating any condition just to alleviate the symptoms without addressing underlying causes. I truly feel anxiety is a natural part of us based on our neurological makeup as described in Chapter 2. I am naturally anxious most of the time. I manage this anxiety by manipulating my environment as much as possible to reduce environmental stressors associated with living in society. I have taught myself to recognize when my anxiety levels begin to increase through body awareness of such signals as feeling my stomach get tense, rapid speech, finger flapping, or fixating on worrying about some potential problem in going off a script I am employing at the moment. I can often behaviorally manage the rising anxiety but there are also many times when unexpected circumstances arise where I cannot self regulate my anxiety, like missing a connecting flight while flying home from a speaking engagement. To be honest, missing a connecting flight in today's overbooked airline industry instantly puts me in such a state of duress and anxiety I doubt any level of anti-anxiety medication would help. I don't think a tranquilizer dart gun sufficient to take down an elephant would reduce my anxiety level in that situation. In those circumstances I find the best "medication" to reduce my out of control anxiety level is to guarantee a seat on the next flight to my missed destination. That instantly greatly reduces my anxiety level and calms me down.

My biggest fear is that there is a tendency to over-medicate our children for behavioral issues. I am particularly concerned for the child who is put on anti-anxiety medications at an early age and left on them for years, if not decades. Subduing the symptoms doesn't allow the individual to learn to recognize their own body signals of rising anxiety or give them an opportunity to learn to self regulate, manage, and control their environment later on in life. Medications often take the place of more intense behavioral management training for the child because now they aren't as "unmanageable" in the school setting. What about the child who has been on anti-anxiety medication since they were eight years old and ten years later, as an adult, decides to refuse any further anxiety medication. I have seen instances where because the medication was so effective there was no emphasis on self awareness and self regulation for the autistic individual. My concern is that when they decide to stop the medication after a prolonged time period they won't have the experience, understanding, and self training in dealing with handling anxiety.

To be honest, I have tried anti-anxiety medications for an eight-month period. My doctor prescribed them for me due to my severe anxiety "attacks" (her term not mine) in airports. Right from the start they did nothing to help reduce my anxiety when complications arose at the airport. After she quadrupled the dosage, still with no visible results, I decided the side effects outweighed any potential yet unseen benefits of continuing its usage so I decreased the dosage over a two-week period until I was finally weaned off. For two weeks after that I had horrible physical withdrawal symptoms of dizziness and imbalance.

This doesn't mean that there aren't autistic individuals who would benefit from these medications. Other influences besides autism should be considered in determining whether medication should be employed, such as a death in the family, personal disaster, or tragedy of any sort, or co-morbid conditions. Medication may help some individuals and if it does those individuals are very fortunate. I tend to be more cynical because I advocate medication as a last resort and see it employed as a first resort. I am a behaviorist at heart who feels that teaching an individual to self regulate and modulate their behaviors through understanding how anxiety impacts their body and mind personally is empowering. Through the use of coping strategies and tools which empower the individual to take control of their life and modify their environment in such a way as to reduce anxiety levels as much as possible, anxiety can be managed but not extinguished and should be embraced and not feared. In the end it comes down to the issue of personal choice based on many factors, not just autism.

There is no easy answer to this controversial issue. It is my sincerest desire to see parents weigh all the factors involved in medicating any child and to consider it only after other behavioral methods have failed. Parents should never feel pressured or strong armed by school officials, or anyone else for that matter. I can personally testify that I have been pressured to go on medication to relieve my anxiety not only by people I knew on a personal level but also from those I sought services from such as dentistry and medicine, and even my former employers. These individuals wouldn't be around to help with other coping strategies that would take time and practice. All they wanted was a quick fix so that they didn't have to deal with my anxiety, which in most cases was due to how they interacted with me. Without truly understanding autism it was impossible for them to see it any other way.

CHAPTER 4

Rituals and Routines: A Natural Defense for Anxiety

Routines are something all human beings engage in and they are an important part of our daily life, starting from a morning routine and continuing right through the day. Whether it is reading the morning paper during breakfast or engaging in some form of exercise such as jogging or yoga, successful completion of these routines seems to set the tone for the day. Routines are also vital in keeping order within society. Businesses and service-based industries depend on routine to ensure peaceful working conditions and an uninterrupted flow of productive work. In the United States the law guarantees employees working an eight-hour day at least a half hour lunch period and two 15-minute breaks during that time. Generally speaking most companies will set the lunch, morning, and afternoon break times based on their need to function effectively. Particularly large establishments such as a hospital may even stagger these times among employees to ensure an orderly continuity of services. Could you imagine the consequences if every hospital employee from the nursing staff down to the food services staff took their lunch and break time either at the same time as everyone else or just randomly when they felt like it? It would create a sense of panic and chaos because that break in the accepted routine would disrupt the entire operation of the hospital. The same goes for when employees decide to strike in protest of some perceived unfairness in their working environment. In a bus strike where no buses run this break in routine negatively impacts many commuters whose routine is to use the bus as a means of transportation to get to and from work. Why is it that when this happens people affected become upset, anxious, and angry when there are other forms of transportation still available such as taxis, bicycles, personal vehicles, and even walking? It is because the routine of taking the bus ensured a smooth transition from home to work or wherever they were going. The routine of taking the bus was so predictable it didn't require any thought, so it brought a sense of order and structure to that timeframe. Many people relax during that time staring blankly out the window, reading the paper or texting on the cell phone because they "feel" no need to guard against not arriving at their destination because the bus travels on a routine schedule. People look forward to their routine coffee or cigarette breaks, leisure activities and outings, and meal times. Routines aid in allowing us an overall sense of calm and well being. This is an overpowering need shared by non autistic individuals and autistic individuals alike. Needing routine and structure doesn't make a person any more or less autistic; it just makes them human.

When I was first diagnosed with high functioning autism the psychologist asked if I engaged in any routines or rituals above and beyond what was considered "normal." I emphatically said no but my friend who accompanied me interrupted and challenged my answer. When I asked my friend for specifics she listed off quite a few rituals and routines just off the top of her head. I honestly felt my "idiosyncrasies" or "quirks" were shared by many people but a thorough analysis revealed they were so particular and meticulous in their execution that indeed they went beyond the reasonable definition of normal. Not being able to execute any one of them put me into a near state of panic. Engaging in them allowed an inner sense of peace.

The need for predictability

Rituals and routines in autism are paramount in maintaining our sense of calmness through predictability. A lack of structure in any part of our daily life breeds anxiety, nervousness, and near paranoia over the unknown because we cannot cope with unpredictability and chaos. Routines and rituals are our number one coping strategy in dealing with daily stressors and anxiety. We know we don't have power over controlling how the world functions, so to deal with life's unpredictability and this lack of control we create our own routines and rituals where we are the "masters of this universe" and can control every aspect of how they are performed. It is a method of creating order out of chaos. When we create a routine or ritual it gives us a sense of control because it is unchanging and predictable and repetition solidifies this. Needing their time scripted autistic individuals are born with an innate craving for routines and rituals and will seek to establish them whenever possible. Engaging in a routine allows us to "feel" safe.

Unfortunately routines can also become non functional and even enslaving to other individuals who are incorporated into a routine. There is a fine line in allowing routines and rituals to ensure an autistic individual's inner sense of well being and having them become so rigid that even the slightest deviation creates a near hysterical response. Just which routine should be allowed and how many are considered beneficial will be dependent on many factors, based on the uniqueness of every individual. There has to be a balance. If you want to be a productive member of society as an autistic person you can't expect the world to conform to your every routine. There will have to be compromises and just plain tolerance for times when routines cannot be followed or are altered. Routines do differ from rituals even though many people interchange the two words so it is important to understand that there can be a difference in both of these natural major anxiety coping techniques. Routines enable us to maintain our scripted timeframes in a predictable and orderly fashion which is calming, whereas rituals aid in reducing anxiety over a particular stressor. They often overlap and it is often very difficult to distinguish between the two because the differences can be so minor and subtle. In this chapter I am going to focus on routines and rituals as they apply to anxiety and meltdowns.

I had in the past felt that although I needed scripts I didn't fall into the category of needing every minute scripted, as I discussed in an earlier chapter. I thought about how I routinely drove once every week to visit a friend who lived two hours away. While driving to my friend's house I wasn't worried about scripting every minute during that time so surely such intense scripting had to be limited to the severely autistic individual. However, once during this driving routine I discovered that I too fell into the category of needing every minute scripted. I had driven there so many times I was accustomed to how long it would take and I noted landmarks at certain time intervals throughout my travels. It was summer and the highway was undergoing road repairs so one lane out of the two lane road was closed. Cars had to creep past a five-mile stretch at no more than 10 miles per hour as opposed to the regular speed limit of 65 miles per hour. This snarled traffic to the point of causing a traffic jam for many miles. I realized at one point that I had not reached the landmark I normally did at my appointed time along the route. I began to feel anxious as now my usual arrival time would be later than I predicted cutting into my allotted time for visiting. Sitting there just waiting for the cars ahead to move was unbearable because I had unscripted time. I didn't know if I would be stuck waiting five minutes or five hours. My routine was interrupted by this delay and because I had not planned on it I didn't bother to script in contingency plans to avoid driving that route. There was absolutely nothing I could do but sit and wait it out. I remember feeling complete helplessness with each passing minute because I had no script to follow and I didn't know what to do to pass the time.

Although every individual is different, routines are universal

Every person with autism is different and perhaps some Asperger's types may disagree with me on the issue of needing every minute scripted, but I truly believe it is an unconscious need that we may not be aware of until a routine falls apart. Even leisure time or down time which may appear as unscripted is still on some level scripted in our mind. Routines are designed to bring us a sense of calm because they are predictable and the repetitive nature of doing something the same way every time is soothing as it allows us to feel a certain amount of security in knowing nothing unpredictable will occur within that particular block of time.

Understanding how routines allow us some measure of serenity is useful in understanding why it is so prevalent in autism. Routines, as I stated, center mainly around a block of time, event, or activity.

What is the function of a ritual?

Rituals are particular thoughts, verbalizations, and actions performed in and out of a routine. Sometimes rituals are fear based, where some event triggered a negative response that created such a sense of helplessness that a ritual was instituted to return a feeling of predictability and control. Usually these rituals are performed immediately preceding the event that created this fear. Rituals can also be a mundane everyday sequence of steps carried out to add to predictability and enhance a routine and may not be associated with any traumatizing event.

HOW A RITUAL DIFFERS FROM A ROUTINE

The difference can be subtle but let me illustrate this delineation with the following example. Every time I drive to town, which is about three or four times weekly, I always stop at the doughnut shop on the way home and buy myself an iced coffee drink. It is a reward for having successfully run my errands because my sensory issues create great difficulties for me in stores. That is my routine as it focuses around a specific event (going to town). After the clerk hands the beverage to me I cannot under any circumstance take a sip until I have first cleansed my hands, and wiped off the lid and sides with a pocket hand sanitizer I always carry. If by chance I forgot to carry the sanitizer I would either go to my car to pick up the spare bottle I keep there, or I would purchase some at the same store, or I would wait to drink the beverage when I got home and perform the ritual there. Not performing the ritual would be devastating, as it would also ruin my routine.

Knowing I have this back up plan goes a long way in feeling a sense of control over the unknown in this situation, especially during the winter months when cold and flu germ transmission is at its greatest. I know that this ritual doesn't guarantee that I will never catch a cold but in my mind I feel I have taken control in protecting myself, even if just in that one circumstance. That particular series of steps is a ritual. Both the routine and ritual offer some sense of comfort. Getting the coffee is something to look forward to and is a regular event I can count on. Engaging in the cleansing ritual also affords me some sense of comfort because I feel I have carried out a function that will increase my odds of not picking up cold or flu germs easily transmitted by dirty hands. You may be thinking that this isn't a ritual but just common sense practiced by lots of other people especially during cold and flu season. It crosses over from common sense to a ritual because it requires rigid adherence without any deviation.

COMMON SENSE, OCD, OR A RITUAL?

Let me share an example that best conveys the difference between common sense and a ritual. Say you are at the check-out lane in a store and the cashier sneezes into her hand and then attempts to give you your change back from the transaction with that very same hand. You forgot your hand sanitizer but you need the purchased items and there is a line of people waiting behind you, so you accept the change praying the money she just handed you isn't infested with cold germs and hope for the best. That would be common sense because you try your best to increase your odds of not picking up cold germs through using hand sanitizer but in instances such as this, where you forgot it, it doesn't deter you from finishing the transaction with the cashier.

In that same situation I would not be so "forgiving." I would insist that the cashier utilize the hand sanitizer dispenser (required now in all our major stores) located next to her cash register and then give me different change. If that weren't an option I would insist on speaking to the manager or person in charge before accepting any money, regardless of how long the line is behind me. That crosses over from common sense into a ritual because it requires my strict adherence to it even in this circumstance. I don't worry about what people waiting impatiently behind me are feeling because I am not the one who sneezed into their hand and without any regard for the customer's health tried to give back germ-covered money.

Maybe you are thinking it is not common sense or a ritual but that it is a perfect example of obsessive compulsive disorder or OCD. I am not a psychologist so I am not qualified to discuss OCD at length. I do know that many children on the spectrum have a co-morbid diagnosis of OCD because of such strict ritual engagement. From my reading I have come to understand that OCD rituals are engaged in out of fear something terrible will happen if they don't perform them. The fear is irrational because they can't justify the rationale behind why they are so compulsive in carrying out that particular function and the ritual is often carried out a specific number of times, such as having to rub a bar of soap eight times between the palms of hand during hand washing or saying a word or phrase so many times consecutively. There seems to be no facts associated in the reasoning behind such a ritual. I have spoken with people diagnosed with OCD and have asked them what compels them to engage in these compulsions. Repeatedly I was told that it was fear or anxiety for indefinable reasons that motivated them.

In my case there are facts behind the motivation for this ritual. A television documentary I watched recently detailed how cold and flu germs are transmitted from person to person and then gave practical strategies on how to avoid picking up these viruses. The main intervention was to use hand sanitizer on your hands when in public or around an ill person, before putting your hands anywhere near your face and mouth. I was merely copying what I had seen on television in regard to staying healthy. I wasn't concerned with how many swipes it would take to cleanse around the coffee cup and lid, so if it took once around or twice it didn't matter as long as I knew I cleaned the area completely. My ritual wasn't based on unknown fears but on facts I had learned watching the documentary. The ritual is meticulous because many individuals on the autism spectrum are very detail orientated. Engaging in the ritual is very calming because I feel I have done something (taken control) of an otherwise uncontrollable situation. I know that won't guarantee that I will not pick up a virus but at least I narrowed my chances of that possibility, if even only in my mind. I am no different than many other autistic individuals in the sense that I hate leaving anything to chance.

I am not implying that OCD doesn't exist as a separate diagnosis within the autism spectrum but with rituals it is important to look for the underlying driving force. See if it makes sense. This is particularly important when a new ritual seems to have started up out of nowhere. If it is fear based there will be a need to engage in it just before the point where something last time created anxiety and a sense of lack of control. Usually rituals will be abundant around transitions of any sort. This is the timeframe where unpredictability and the unexpected are at its highest. The more agitated the individual is or becomes the more rigidly and intensely they engage in that particular ritual. They are doing it to take back control over something they were not able to control by creating and performing a certain sequence of actions that they believe to be beneficial. It may not appear useful, logical, or beneficial to anyone else but it is a major coping strategy that brings a sense of calmness to them.

UNEXPLAINABLE RITUALS

What about rituals that cannot be pinpointed to some known anxiety trigger but center around daily living issues such as meal times where the child insists on finishing one food item on their plate completely before moving on to the next? I have seen children whose ritual it is to eat and finish one vegetable at a time in sequential order before moving on to the other items. I have also seen children who cannot bear to have any food items touching each other on their plate. Sometimes rituals are created not out of fear but as a way to exert control when there is too much change or unpredictability going on in that individual's life.

Rituals always reflect a need for security and control over some aspect of daily life no matter how trivial it appears to others. Rituals may not always occur centered around the area of unpredictability for them. A child who is experiencing many changes at school may create numerous seemingly pointless rituals at home in areas where there had never been any difficulties, as a means of dealing with the unpredictability of the school environment. People with autism do not take kindly to sudden change or spontaneity. The changes at school may go undetected by the teacher or parent because they are so subtle.

MINOR CHANGES THAT COULD CREATE ANXIETY, LEADING TO NEW RITUALS AT HOME OR SCHOOL

- Rearranging the furniture in the classroom.

- Switching the seating arrangement of the students in a particular class.

- Losing their self assigned seating arrangement. It is very common for children to pick a certain seat during lunchtime in the cafeteria and expect to sit in it every time even though the seats are available to all students and operate on a first come first sit basis.

- Implementing plans and interventions to correct a certain behavior or extinguish a non functional routine or ritual. Correction of any sort is initially not well tolerated and may lead to an increase of new rituals to compensate.

- Rotating the activities during gym (physical fitness training) class, such as playing soccer for three consecutive weeks and then rotating to basketball for a few weeks and then rotating to another group sport.

- Changes in the bus route or even different drivers. Even in my day it was very common for the school bus driver to break the routine of going the same way and add a new street for children who just moved into the school district area without forewarning.

- Vague statements that aren't concrete enough in terms of timeframes, used frequently, such as "We will see" or "Maybe later." I will cover this in more depth in Chapter 8.

It is important to understand that even non verbal individuals with autism, if they understand language, will react no differently from a verbal child to the above mentioned examples, even though they cannot verbally express themselves. A ritual always brings with it a sense of comfort in its engagement whether the person is verbal or not.

Interrupting routines

Routines tend to create a more intense negative response when altered or broken. Routines more than rituals help in reducing anxiety because routines portion out the day into very concrete timeframes. They allow for less anxiety over the unknown because a routine is unchanging. Abruptly altering or breaking any routine is one of the leading causes of meltdowns. Because autistic individuals need predictability it is a natural tendency for us to seek out patterns of consistency in just about any daily activity. I always say that anything done exactly the same way two or three times in a row will be quickly seen as routine. Routines therefore can be seen as the proverbial double-edged sword. Establishing routines that don't negatively impact on others ensures a sense of calmness, whereas non functional routines established unintentionally will always create a severe negative response when you subsequently try to halt that routine.

NON FUNCTIONAL ROUTINES ESTABLISHED UNINTENTIONALLY

Non functional routines may be established accidently by well meaning parents or professionals working with autistic children. A classic example that I have seen the aftermath of revolves around getting the autistic child to go somewhere in a vehicle. Let's say a mother promises her autistic child that if he behaves in the car on the way to wherever she will stop at his favorite "fast food" restaurant for his favorite snack item. This powerful motivator works so well that the mother decides to offer the same reward the next time her child gets in the vehicle. Seeing this as an effective tool she does this four or five consecutive times whenever she needs her child to go somewhere in the vehicle. After the third time the child incorporates this as part of the "going somewhere in a vehicle routine" based on his or her inclination to look for patterns. In the child's mind it now has become part of the established routine. On the sixth trip out the father is driving instead of the mother and decides that there is not enough time to stop for the expected snack and drives by the restaurant or takes another route to avoid the child noticing his intentions of not stopping. It doesn't take the autistic child long to notice and respond negatively and possibly very strongly to this perceived breach of protocol. The intention behind offering the reward in the first place was good but it quickly developed into a non functional routine because now it was expected every time they drove someplace.

AVOIDING THE USE OF IMMEDIATE TANGIBLE REWARDS

The best way to avoid such a scenario in the first place is by not using food as an immediate reward for any well behaved moments, especially in the non verbal population. I was called in once for a behavioral consult regarding a non verbal child behaving out of control in the classroom. It didn't take long to find the underlying cause of the child's distress. They were using candy as an immediate reward for successful completion of a step for a specific task. It was used as a motivator to teach the child how to perform the task. The child became accustomed to picking out a piece of candy at the various step levels of this task so that it became incorporated as a routine in his mind, part of fulfilling the goal of successfully completing the task. When the teacher decided to no longer offer the candy until after the task was completed the child responded with very strong negative emotions (equivalent to the biblical wailing and gnashing of teeth). As in the previous vehicle example it wasn't the intent of the educators to create a routine within a routine. They were just hoping to enhance the routine.

The strategy I strongly advocate in any behavior modification circumstance is to never offer an immediate edible reward. It encourages a sense of entitlement to instant gratification. I prefer a token system which empowers the child to understand the concept of self regulation of inner anxiety. I have found the token system very effective in teaching responsibility, good work ethics, and self control. I am sure you, the reader, are very familiar with this system as it is not exclusive to autism and is practiced throughout the world. If you work outside of the home then you are engaging in a token system. When you work a five-day work week your employer doesn't give you a reward of some household necessity at the end of each day nor does he leave a large trolley of food at your work station at the end of the work week for you. Instead he hands you a piece of paper called a paycheck which your bank replaces with money, which can also be considered tokens. You then have the opportunity to choose how you wish to spend your money (or tokens) to purchase the items you would like. In order to receive the tokens it requires commitment and the successful completion of a work week. If you choose to not go into work one day and have no personal, vacation, or sick days available you will forfeit a portion of the tokens earned and receive a smaller paycheck that week. This same principle would allow a child to earn a token of sorts for good behavior at predetermined intervals for successful completion of that part of the task. At either the end of the task or day allowing the child to "cash in" the tokens by choosing what reward they would like from a menu board reinforces good behavior and patience. For the much higher functioning child I recommend verbal praise with an oral agreement of some predetermined non tangible reward such as certain allotment of time to engage in their special interest after the task is successfully completed.

I, of all people, understand that routines are critical to our well being but every child with autism will encounter numerous times when routines will fall apart throughout their life. I understand well meaning adults who revolve their lives around the child's routines in order not to provoke any negative behaviors but the child must come to realize that there will be times when this is not possible. Using tangible rewards as a mainstay for enforcing a routine will create an individual who will become demanding. Rather than using bribery as a means of compliance, the individual should have a vast array of coping tools and strategies to use in situations when routines may become altered.

MODIFY A ROUTINE GRADUALLY

Breaking or abruptly altering either a functional or non functional routine will cause distress because it interrupts the pattern of continuity and predictability. Always modify any routine, functional or non functional, slowly over time in small increments so that the individual has a chance to adapt. A sudden disruption in any routine brings severe anxiety because what was once predictable now isn't. Breaking a routine is going off a script. As I mentioned in Chapter 1, going off script is equivalent to jumping out of an airplane without a parachute to a person with autism.

REPLACING A NON FUNCTIONAL ROUTINE

When trying to replace a non functional routine with a functional routine it will require the following action plan:

1. Always discuss that a change will be taking place in advance of actually modifying the routine in question. Never ever under any circumstance make it a surprise unless you want a full blown catastrophic reaction. Create a working script on paper of what is to be encountered and or expected. Explain in detail what is about to occur and reassure them that only a small section of the routine will altered until they are comfortable with it. Let them understand that you are not trying to destroy a routine with nothing to fall back on but that there will be something equally as calming established in its place.

2. If feasible utilize a social story and/or incorporate photos as an identifier of a certain interval within the modified routine so that the individual can get a "mental picture" or visualize what is involved in this new routine. Social stories work best with younger children. With teenagers and adults there may be a tendency for the individual to refute the reasons, rationale, or logic behind the story. I myself will tend to question a social story when utilized on me by asking for many more details and "what if?" scenarios which tends to destroy the purpose of the story by going off track. For me it is best to show a visual time-line picture board with photos of what to expect.

3. Use a motivator or reward for successful completion of certain steps. People with autism are intensely reluctant to change. Special interests or passions are best suited as a motivator tool because it is an area we love to indulge in. It may be the promise of allowing the individual to engage in a specific pleasurable activity at the end of the lesson for Asperger's individuals, or letting a non verbal child play with a favorite toy.

4. For the verbal individual, discuss what coping tools or strategies would be effective during the lesson should something not

go according to script and be sure they are available to the individual to utilize should they become anxious. For the non verbal individual, have stim tools at the ready for calming. Remember the less verbal the individual the slower and smaller the steps must be.

5. Be prepared for tears, a reluctance to continue, or just complete refusal to participate in the modification. To minimize the possibility of failure, always work on modifying any routine when the autistic individual is not stressed or preoccupied with something else. In the proper learning environment stay firm on successful completion in one area and do not back down and allow the lesson to end until a positive result is achieved. (By proper learning environment I mean that the conditions are ideal for the child or adult to stay focused without distractions, so that there is a calmness and not a sense of urgency to work on the lesson which the child or adult may sense and then become stressed over.)

6. Remember: small increments. Do not attempt to change a non functional routine overnight. It will take time and patience on your part.

7. Most importantly once you have communicated how a routine will unfold *do not* deviate from that under any circumstance without giving prior warning of unforeseen variables and having alternate scripts should they occur. Let us use the shopping example from an earlier chapter where autistic Timmy is required to go to the grocery store with his mother to pick up some milk. In that situation the mother scripted out in detail how the activity would unfold saying that she was only going in to purchase some milk and eggs. It is extremely common for everyone to decide at one time or another, once inside the store, "Well while I am here I might as well pick up a few other things." If you have not communicated that in advance, and your autistic child notices you going after more than just milk and eggs, it will be interpreted as a complete break in the

script. The routine here is that the mother always completely discussed her intentions and actions when going food shopping ahead of going so that Timmy could get a visual of what to expect. She did not add possible "plan Bs" or alternate scripts should a deviation need to occur. Her shopping for other items in this instance conveys to the individual, whether child or adult, that she cannot be trusted. I know it sounds harsh but that is the truth. If you have a habit of altering a script even just slightly, but abruptly, rituals will become more prevalent as the individual tries to cope with your perceived inability to follow an established order.

HANDLING INTERRUPTIONS IN ROUTINES

A much better approach that I can honestly say will teach Timmy that there may be times when routines will have to abruptly change for unforeseen circumstances is to have reserve or back up scripts to utilize in that situation. What becomes so devastating in something as simple as going after other items other than the predetermined milk and eggs is the fact that the script failed and there was no back up plan, which meant from that point forward there was no way to predict the timeline of the event. Needing every minute scripted whether we are conscious of that or not comes out in these situations. Without a plan Timmy feels as if he was thrown out of that plane without a parachute, and now he falls helplessly into the unknown. In this store example the deviation was also a choice made by the mother. People with autism are very literal. If you begin not to do exactly what you say, it will, over time, lead to non functional routines or rituals as a coping method to handle your communication. In this particular instance it would have been best to just get the milk and eggs and leave.

UNFORESEEN INTERRUPTIONS IN A ROUTINE

What about unforeseen interruptions in the grocery store of someone, a neighbor or friend, coming up to the mother and wanting to talk to her? I actually learned a phrase that I incorporate as a back up response from flying so often. Before the plane leaves the gate the flight attendant always gives us a safety briefing of what to do in an emergency. The standard phrase spoken when talking about using the seat as a flotation device is, "In the unlikely event of a water landing your seat cushion doubles as a flotation device." Script in potential deviations with the phrase, "In the unlikely event of..."

With Timmy, if the mother scripts in, "In the unlikely event I run into someone who knows me and wants to talk I will tell them I have you with me and we are on a tight schedule and I cannot stop to talk, or I will talk for five minutes and you can time it by your watch." Convey whatever you would do in that possible deviation ahead of time and have alternate plans for just such an occasion.

Reality dictates that there will be numerous times throughout life when routines will be broken or deviated from due to unforeseen circumstances and a plan B or alternate script isn't available. Let's say you are taking your son to his weekly soccer practices and create a routine where you will leave a half hour earlier than needed so as to get an ice cream before reaching the soccer field. It has become a fun routine where the two of you have some quality alone time to just talk. It something you look forward to as well. On this latest trip out there is an auto accident up ahead on the road you are driving on. The road is completely impassable. There are vehicles in front of and behind you so there is nowhere for you to go. It is obvious that not only will there be no time for ice cream but getting to the soccer field late is a reality. Your son becomes visibly anxious and starts obsessing on how he will not get to play soccer. This is a distressing situation for anyone, but if you add to the misery by complaining, whining, or even swearing, your autistic child will pick up on the negativity and his anxiety level will dramatically rise. No matter how excitable your child becomes it is crucial to stay calm and talk in a low even tone.

In situations like these where there is no alternative and the autistic individual has to endure the situation it is paramount that they utilize calming strategies. If your child has an object that they find extremely calming when anxious make sure to always pack it in the vehicle just in case you encounter an unforeseen circumstance that causes duress to your child. It may be a toy, or favorite stim tool, or iPod with music, for example. It could also be a sensory item that soothes their anxiety. Maybe it is something as simple as playing a word game in the car to refocus on something other than having gone off script. The possibilities are endless and depend on the individual. It is very important that you know what calms the anxiety of the individual you are around and have those items and strategies available for them. The long term goal is self regulation of anxiety as much as possible. This is done through utilizing self coping skills in these types of situations over time. In time they will come to recognize that while they don't like being in these circumstances there is no alternative so they must learn to cope with the moment and engage in something constructive that will lessen their anxiety.

The influence of stress on routines and rituals

The more stressed an autistic person is the more strongly they will engage in either a ritual or routine, or both. If it almost appears compulsive it is a definitive sign that the individual is desperately trying to normalize their environment through predictability by repetitively engaging in either an action or thought continuously. They are doing this to calm themselves down. I strongly advocate that anyone who is present when an autistic individual is stressed should just allow engagement of a harmless ritual or routine if it means that they can then move forward through a stressor. It is counterproductive to get into an argument or battle which will only serve to stress the autistic person further and intensify their wanting to perform the ritual or routine you are trying to interrupt.

A PERSONAL EXAMPLE OF HOW A NON FUNCTIONAL ROUTINE WAS CALMING

I can best convey this point of allowing non harmful rituals in order to cope with severe anxiety by a situation that occurred to me two years ago. It was a hot and humid August afternoon and my husband and I had been working on fixing farm machinery so that we could hay our fields. Both of us were sweaty and covered in dirt and oil. I went into the barn to fetch some machinery tools and while I reached in the tool box my wrist caught the sharp tip of a manure-splattered hoof paring knife. It punctured my wrist through the tendon. As it began to bleed profusely I knew that I would require medical care. I have a history of going to the emergency room at our local hospital with each visit ending in a disaster, with miscommunications leading me into full meltdowns. This is so stressful I choose not to go unless it is life threatening because even though I tell them I have autism, because I look "normal" and am educated they do not believe me. Just the mere thought of knowing I would have to go to the hospital created angst in every fiber of my being. When I am injured or very ill I become quiet and tend to seek isolation. I don't panic or let my emotions show.

When I looked at the injury I just sat down, took off my shoe and sock, and made the sock into a makeshift tourniquet around my wrist. I calmly walked out to where my husband was working and asked if he would stop what he was doing and consider an impromptu trip to town. My husband knows that I have a routine for going to town and such an impromptu trip was out of character for me. Immediately he asked what was wrong to which I responded that I might have injured myself beyond the limited capabilities of my medical knowledge. When I showed him the injury he panicked because (admittedly) there was a lot of blood running down my hand and pooling on the ground. As he ran into the house to get the car keys he told me to get in the vehicle. I said I can't go until I shower. He began to argue saying I could die from blood loss so there is no time to waste. I countered with the fact that I knew I didn't cut an artery so I wasn't in immediate danger of bleeding to death. In my routine for going to see a doctor for any reason I have a ritual that I always perform and to ignore this ritual for any reason is unthinkable. That ritual is to take a bath or shower and put on clean clothes before leaving the house. I engage in this ritual because I know my visits will end unfavorably and at least by going clean I feel like I have taken control of one tiny aspect of an unpleasant uncontrollable encounter. To me it is not negotiable. It is calming because it is predictable and monotonous. This is a classic example of where it is best to consider the ramifications of insisting on not allowing a ritual.

My husband became visibly distraught at the realization that the more he pressured me to forget engaging in it "just this one time," the more anxious I became, which created a deeper need to perform the ritual. Looking at the options his choice was to stand his ground, so we would be there for hours arguing, or simply allow the five extra minutes it would take for me to shower and change clothes. His goal was to get to the hospital as quickly as possible so waiting five minutes was more logical than standing around and arguing for 30 minutes, especially since I was unable to listen to reason. This situation was serious and possibly life threatening. Even though my husband felt my bathing ritual was inappropriate it wasn't the place for a confrontation over not allowing what seemed to him a non functional but harmless ritual. He did try to reason with me initially but the anxiety I was experiencing over what I would anticipate at the hospital diminished my cognitive and reasoning abilities. As the anxiety level increases, the body gears more towards the instinctual fight or flight response thereby decreasing cognitive functioning skills. An autistic individual who is visibly stressed and resorting to rituals or routines as a way to cope with the situation is not in a rational state of mind to listen to reason. During such times it is not wise to attempt to reason or expect explanations of why they are insistent on engaging in that behavior. It is not an act of defiance but a means for regaining a sense of control. If it is a harmless ritual or routine but may delay your schedule a little bit, remember it is a coping strategy to reduce anxiety. Forcing them to do otherwise will only encourage a full blown meltdown. Always work on changing a ritual or routine you feel inappropriate when the person isn't stressed and never while they are in a stressful situation.

Never interfere with a ritual or routine

I must in conclusion stress that well intended attempts to engage in a ritual or routine with the autistic person who is stressed as a means of communicating solidarity and empathy will severely adversely affect the ability of the autistic person to calm down. Why?

The answer is: unpredictability.

Routines or rituals are all about engaging in a behavior or activity that is predictable and unchanging. When you inject yourself into that routine or ritual you become an unknown variable that changes the predictable outcome. It is no longer predictable and will actually create more anxiety in the individual because they cannot control your actions. It is no longer a ritual or routine because the outcome cannot be anticipated to be the same as it always was. Stand back and monitor the routine or ritual from a safe distance where you can allow them the personal space to calm down, yet be present should you need to intervene in unforeseen circumstances.

CHAPTER 5

What is a Meltdown?

In this chapter I am going to do what no one can do unless they have autism, and that is to explain what we are thinking and feeling as we spiral into a meltdown. What goes through our minds during a meltdown? Why do we not seem to feel pain during this event? What happens during a meltdown phase? What is it like for a person experiencing a meltdown? Why do we lose awareness of our surroundings? What do we feel immediately afterwards?

Not all individuals will experience meltdowns

I must emphasize that meltdowns will occur in individuals with autism but a percentage don't seem to have visible episodes or are not plagued by them at all. Meltdowns are not a requirement for being autistic. The exact opposite can occur, where instead of having obvious outward behaviors showing distress the individual has a shut down where they completely disengage from the world around them. The key is to remember that people with autism are individuals and while I will discuss meltdown signs and symptoms it is by no means designed to apply to every individual. Each individual will experience symptoms unique to them so it is very important that you are familiar with that person's triggers and responses. This book along with every other book on autism should be a guide that gives you general information on how best to understand and deal with certain areas of autism. Please do not assume that any book, mine included, will exactly explain what every individual with autism experiences. There are factors beyond autism, be they cultural, environmental, and family, that heavily influence behavior. However, that being said, all meltdowns have certain signs and symptoms in common with each other in every autistic individual who experiences meltdowns.

Meltdowns are *not* tantrums

Meltdowns seem to create the biggest concern when addressing issues specific to autism. I cannot tell you how many books I read or seminars I attended that interchanged the word meltdown with tantrum when explaining the extreme negative behavioral responses of an autistic person. This may be seen as pedantic but I even differentiate between meltdowns and catastrophic reactions because there is a noticeable difference in their onset. Meltdowns and catastrophic reactions are involuntary responses while tantrums are purposeful manipulations of behavior to achieve an intended end result. Whereas meltdowns are an unconscious reaction, tantrums are a voluntary choice. Understanding the difference between a meltdown and tantrum is critical because the interventions are completely opposite, and using the wrong strategy will only worsen the situation in both cases. I have decided to split meltdowns and tantrums into two separate chapters so that I can fully detail both experiences to help you better understand why it is important to distinguish tantrums from meltdowns before attempting an intervention.

What is a meltdown?

I am somewhat saddened that there still seems to be such misunderstanding regarding meltdowns. In dealing with behaviors one cannot just concentrate on symptom repression by either the use of medication or behavioral plans without fully comprehending the meltdown complex. Outward signs or symptoms of increasing anxiety are a sort of language that articulates clearly what the individual is feeling internally. Meltdowns are not a maladaptive response pattern to overwhelming stressors but an instinctual adaptation to these stressors, so trying to correct behaviors during a meltdown will only result in failure. Life always finds a way to survive and adapt to harsh environments: trees manage to grow and thrive on the sheer face of a mountain, the polar bear lives in the uninhabitable arctic region. So too autistic individuals have found ways to "adapt" into a society that can be a harsh environment by engaging in instinctual "adaptations," but when these adaptations (coping strategies) are not allowed the situation will inevitably unfavorably resolve itself through a meltdown. A lot of focus seems to be put on post meltdown strategies to prevent future meltdowns but I can tell you honestly that is not entirely possible. The only way to minimize future episodes is by pre-meltdown strategies. Post meltdown strategies implemented immediately or shortly after a meltdown episode are as effective as shutting the barn door after the horses have escaped from their stalls and bolted. To effectively deal with meltdowns in a child or adult you must be proactive and not reactive.

How I developed my interest in creating meltdown interventions

I became extremely focused on developing an understanding of the meltdown complex and proper interventions shortly after my diagnosis of high functioning autism in 2005 at the age of 44. All my life I had been plagued with explosive reactive behavioral responses often over seemingly trivial issues to those around me.

They happened mainly in public places despite the aversion I have for drawing attention to myself for inappropriate behaviors. Ironically when I was alone I noticed that these extreme responses were greatly reduced and limited to unforeseeable changes that interrupted my immediate plans. The general reaction I received from those witnessing these episodes was of my being "overly dramatic" and "selfish" by insisting things had to "always go my way." I knew I was giving the wrong impression but I was completely unable to control my actions. Afterwards I always felt so devastated and humiliated that I began to avoid social contact for fear of having a meltdown misinterpreted as a deliberate bid for attention.

Three months before being diagnosed with autism I decided to see a therapist for help in developing social skills which I hoped would reduce or completely eliminate meltdowns in public. Ironically I began to have an increase in meltdowns during this time with the therapist, so much so that I ended up bringing a new friend with me during these sessions to help understand what was going wrong. Luckily she had a son recently diagnosed with Asperger's Syndrome and was familiar with my literal concrete communication style and had already in her mind diagnosed me with autism. The therapist had a wonderful success rate with helping people but wasn't well experienced in dealing with autistic adults. As a matter of fact I was his first adult on the spectrum. High functioning forms of autism in adults weren't as well recognized then as they are today. Most of the focus was on children with Asperger's and there was then, as still lingers today, a mistaken belief that it is only dysfunctional in children. Compounding this erroneous belief is the notion that, because we look normal and appear to be able to function somewhat in society, higher functioning forms of autism can be outgrown as adults.

My friend was instrumental in pointing out to the therapist and me during the session that I did not understand what was being conveyed. My escalating behaviors in his office were all due to communication difficulties and misinterpretation of the definition and use of words. It was agreed that I needed further evaluation from a more qualified professional experienced in testing adults for a variety of disorders, ranging from mental illnesses to autism. Although I was never successful in obtaining any valuable social skills during my short lived social skills training sessions I did, however, begin to understand how miscommunications can quickly develop into meltdowns. This was further illustrated when I went for my testing three months later to see if I was in fact autistic or afflicted with some mental disorder. At that time I still did not believe that I was autistic but just gifted verbally in a world that didn't bother to adhere to a word's definition as defined by a dictionary. I used to argue constantly with anyone who didn't apply logic or reason to a certain situation but acted emotionally and irrationally because of it. I felt that I was right and the world was wrong.

In Chapter 2 I described how neuro-psychological testing led me to my "freeze," and subsequent meltdowns. As a result of this experience I left the tester's office committed to exploring how I could better comprehend how and when such episodes would likely occur and what I could do to minimize them. Initially it was strictly a self serving endeavor but as I began to explore autistic meltdowns I realized that so many individuals like me had just as great a difficulty in controlling themselves in overwhelming or overstimulating situations. I started reading books specifically written for addressing meltdowns and the strategies that were recommended seemed totally inappropriate, with punitive overtones. In essence many of the books were disciplining us for behaviors and reactions beyond our control. I talked to many parents and individuals on the spectrum and found out that I wasn't alone in being misinterpreted as tantruming during a meltdown. During this period I had sustained an injury requiring immediate medical attention at our local hospital and that visit, like all those before, ended up in a meltdown with me feeling humiliated and the staff seeing me as mentally ill. I contacted the local autism society chapter for my state knowing they offered free autism awareness training, asking if they had any training programs for emergency room (ER) personnel in how to deal properly with an autistic individual who was in an anxious state. They had no such training for meltdowns but after expressing my concerns they asked if I would be willing to create a training program especially designed to help medical professionals better interact with autistic individuals so as to avoid potential meltdowns. Who better to work on such a program then a person with autism with a master's degree in education?

I agreed and my ER training program was a success. I began traveling, first around the state and then around the country, teaching professionals of all sorts how to understand and deal with meltdowns. Requests to come to various agencies as a consultant to help in dealing with meltdowns and behaviors became numerous. So successful was this that I expanded on this training program to include anyone responding to a meltdown whether a doctor, baby sitter, teacher or teacher's aide, or clerk at the grocery store. With the help of a co-author this information was compiled into *Managing Meltdowns: Using the S.C.A.R.E.D. Calming Technique with Children and Adults with Autism*, which was published in 2009 by Jessica Kingsley Publishers. Designed to be used during a meltdown in real time to de-escalate the situation it was brief and to the point. I quickly realized that while extremely informative and full of practical strategies it did little to fully explain the dynamics of a meltdown verses a tantrum and offered only a little glimpse into how we process the world around us, which is a very valuable key in understanding how to prevent meltdowns. Consider this book you are reading now as an adjunct to the meltdown book because it will give the insights required to fully appreciate what we as autistic people experience during this stressful time and better appreciate the strategies in my first book.

What causes a meltdown?

Meltdowns are extreme emotional and/or behavioral responses to a stressful situation. They are *always* involuntary. Meltdowns come from prolonged exposure to sensory triggers or cognitive overload without any chance to get away from the overwhelming stimulation. Usually there will be signs of increasing frustration with accompanying anxiety that slowly starts to escalate if the situation is ignored. Catastrophic reactions on the other hand are explosive immediate involuntary reactions to something having gone off script or not according to plan. One moment the individual is content and the very next completely out of control with no forewarning of such an intense reaction. While I differentiate between a meltdown and a catastrophic reaction based on onset, there is no other major differentiating characteristic between the two. Being autistic I am very precise in my word definitions. The interventions are identical. Some people prefer one term over another and for everyday usage interchanging the two words to describe the same reaction is of little significance in practical applications.

GOING OFF SCRIPT: A LEADING CAUSE OF MELTDOWNS AND CATASTROPHIC REACTIONS

Why do they occur? There are varied reasons for this. Catastrophic or immediate powerful negative responses come primarily from something going off script or not going according to plan. It is not being able to comprehend the reasoning for such an abrupt change or not having a back up script. For instance let's say you take your autistic son "Timmy" to the swimming pool every Tuesday afternoon at the local gym club. To avoid any potential meltdowns, just before leaving you call to make sure the pool is open that afternoon. You reassure your autistic son that the pool is in fact open as you just called to confirm that fact so the plan is to drive to the gym. This is his highlight of the day and he eagerly anticipates being able to play in the water. All is well until you arrive. There is a handwritten note on the door saying, "Sorry for the inconvenience but the pool is closed today." Completely caught off guard your son immediately escalates into an extreme negative response complete with wailing and head banging. Your attempts to calm him down by offering to go tomorrow to make up for today is met with increased anxiety and more tears. His reaction goes beyond being disappointed right into being completely devastated over this occurrence. It is a catastrophic reaction that had no prior build up of anxiety due to a stressor and came out of nowhere. Why? What happened?

Little autistic Timmy didn't understand the reason for such an abrupt change of plans. The note offered no concrete explanation to why it was closed. More importantly the reason Timmy went into such an extreme response was because he went off script. Remember I talked about how going off script was as terrifying as jumping out of a plane without a parachute and how we crave for every waking minute to be scripted? The plan or script was to go swimming. That timeframe of swimming was a block of time scripted out in terms of duration of the activity and time to and from the location. The rest of the afternoon into evening became scripted out based on the plan of going swimming. Now suddenly there is this void filled instead with unscripted time throwing off every other script that followed this activity for the rest of the day. It doesn't matter whether your child has the ability to tell time or not, most children verbal or non verbal have a good working concept of the duration of a pleasurable activity. If you do not believe me, try cutting short a fun activity routinely engaged in with an autistic person and watch their reaction. I have been around non verbal children who couldn't tell time but had a better concept of timeframes from repetitive engagement in a pleasurable activity or routine than even myself.

Now Timmy has no working script for this timeframe that should have been occupied with water activities. This empty time slot is now unpredictable and unscriptable. Unpredictability breeds terror and terror leads to uncontrollable instinctual reactions of self preservation.

NOT RECEIVING COMPREHENDIBLE ANSWERS: ANOTHER MAJOR SOURCE OF MELTDOWNS

Meltdowns can occur as the result of not getting clarification or comprehendible answers to questions. Non definable phrases such as "Maybe later," or "I will be with you shortly" have no beginning or ending. It is to us a state of limbo or suspension because there is no definable timeframe. Even the word "no" will elicit a meltdown in some individuals, particularly the non verbal, because it is a word that isn't descriptive. This is exactly what happened during my neuro-psychological testing, when I asked the tester to clarify the vague instructions on how to complete the subtest I was working on. Remember, the only response she was allowed to give was that in order not to contaminate the results she could only repeat the question. That wasn't an answer because it didn't address "why" it wasn't allowed. I needed to know beforehand why and how just clarifying the instructions would dramatically alter test results. Although after all the testing was completed she did carefully explain why in detail, which then made logical sense, it was too late to be of any use in preventing the meltdown.

Two types of meltdown/catastrophic reaction: cognitive and sensory meltdowns

There are two types of meltdown or catastrophic reaction: cognitive and sensory.

COGNITIVE MELTDOWNS

As I stated earlier autistic individuals are problem solvers; we need logical concrete answers and will focus a great deal of time and energy trying to come up with likely solutions to something distressing. Being impulsive by nature, many on the spectrum will "obsess" on the worst case scenario because of a tendency to jump to conclusions before having all the facts. As their brains try desperately to find a logical response, commonly they will overthink the problem, creating a cognitive overload because their reasoning is based only on what information they can surmise and not all the facts. Cognitive overload also results from too many unclear verbal instructions or open ended questions, pushing up the frustration level because they don't understand what is being asked of them. Most cognitive overloads occur either because something went off script or there were miscommunications.

Cognitive overload and meltdowns

Cognitive overload leads to a meltdown. Why? It is because the brain is overworking trying to find a resolution to the problem but creates only endless possibilities that can't be verified at that moment. It is very similar to a computer freeze or crash. Have you ever when sending an email hit the send key and watched nothing happen? If you are like me (very impatient) or a new computer user you hit the key again. Still nothing happens, so in frustration you hit the send key twenty times in rapid succession. The little arrow icon becomes an hourglass and on the top of the screen pops a message that your computer is not responding. In effect the computer froze because you didn't give it time to process the initial request, it then didn't understand what you were asking, so you "badgered" it to move forward by continually pressing the send key. The only way to get it responding again is to shut off the computer and restart it so it can reboot. This is very similar to what happens in the autistic brain during a cognitive meltdown. The brain becomes so cognitively overloaded it can't function anymore so it "shuts down" and the instinctual self preservation mode takes over. We have no control at that point.

The first system to fail is our communication abilities. On some level most of us who experience meltdowns know we are losing our cognitive functioning, so in a desperate attempt to override that we try harder to communicate before losing communication ability. Ironically that only increases the pressure and overload so the brain shuts down even further. I have seen first hand the look of panic and even terror on an individual's face when they are spiraling into a meltdown. It truly unnerves me because I understand that they are desperately trying to halt the progression of a meltdown but with impaired cognitive functioning it is beyond any self regulation at that point. The feeling is one of inner helplessness and desperation. Somehow you know you will lose most if not all awareness of your surroundings. You will be at the mercy of those around you without any ability to self advocate.

As this sense of panic increases it triggers the fight or flight response which will effectively shut down all cognitive processing and resort to a primal instinctual self preservation mode. During this phase the individual will not be able to recognize those around them including parents, siblings, caregivers, or teachers. It is very scary for us. This is the dangerous point where interveners tend to get hurt if they try to touch or restrain an individual in that state. During this period individuals may seem to "black out" or be completely unaware of who they are, where they are, time, and the situation. To complicate this phase even further the pain threshold tends to rise so dramatically that individuals who engage in self injurious behavior, those being physically restrained, or those in a surrounding causing physical harm will not be aware of or register any pain. This is due to the fight or flight inhibition of pain responses so that the individual can either escape to safety or have the strength to fight for their life.

This is the point where an autistic person can be seriously injured yet not show any distress until after the meltdown has ended, the point where a person with autism can die at the hands of another. If you try to forcibly physically restrain an individual in this state they will fight even harder to free themselves because, remember, they are totally unaware of who you are. All they are registering at that moment is that some outside force is trying to harm them, so they must fight back to protect themselves. Telling them repeatedly who you are and that you are just trying to help will not register to them because cognitive functioning has been suspended for that duration. It is very easy to asphyxiate an autistic person through restraint to the point of death without realizing it because the individual is increasing their efforts to break free. That is the fight response.

Too much choice causing a meltdown

Meltdowns also tend to occur when there are too many choices given to an individual, even if they are pleasurable. For instance, you decide to take autistic Timmy to the toy store as a reward for having successfully completed some major goal. You tell him he can pick any toy in the store. Timmy's all excited and happy but as soon as you enter the store and he sees the vast array of items to choose from he breaks down into tears. Despite this supposed pleasurable activity a cognitive overload occurred over how to break down the possibilities into only one choice.

Cognitive overload over too many choices also occurred to me when I first began speaking on autism. I had gotten used to speaking for two hours with a 15-minute break half way through my presentations. During break time it was customary to partake in the free beverages offered by the hosting agency. I had done about a half dozen presentations by that time and the refreshments were always limited to tea or coffee, two or three juice choices, and some soft drinks. Because I had the same consistency regarding beverage choices where I presented in the past, I quickly (and erroneously) assumed every presentation would offer roughly the same variety of drinks. Once while speaking at a university when it was time for the refreshment break I walked over to the refreshment table. As I was the speaker the attendees allowed me to be the first in line to get a beverage. Expecting the usual fare I was so completely taken by surprise at the choice of drinks available. There were at least a dozen different juices, teas of all descriptions, flavored and unflavored coffees, and a huge variety of different soft drinks. I was so stunned by the amount of choice I was unable to process what I saw. I froze, unable to think or move. The person who accompanied me to this presentation saw my dilemma and reacted quickly but calmly, resolving what could have been a meltdown. When she saw that I was "stuck" all she did was pick up two likely choices, place them in front of my face, and stated simply, "Deb, apple or orange juice?"

That command was enough to redirect my thoughts over how was I possibly going to be able to choose just one drink and focus only on what was directly in front of me. I was able to choose from just two selections and the entire situation resolved itself without incident. Now had this person started to badger me when it was clear I was unable to make a choice with something like, "Hurry up, Deb, there are people waiting behind you. You are holding up the line so just choose. Come on, what are you waiting for?"

That response would have pushed my frustration level beyond what I could handle because I cognitively couldn't process how to make a selection. With so many choices my brain needed a lot more time to figure out how to narrow down the choice of drinks on my own. The badgering would have increased the pressure for me to cognitively function when it was clear I was cognitively impaired. A badgering response would have led to a meltdown.

Bolting or running away during a meltdown

Sometimes individuals will bolt or run away during a meltdown. It occurs for the same reason as the fight response…it is instinctual. The instinctual preservation mode is triggered sending them fleeing away from the stressful situation. This too is a particularly dangerous phase in the meltdown for the same safety concerns. At this point there is no cognitive processing or functioning going on in the brain, only an uncontrollable urge to flee for safety. Individuals who are "bolters" or runaways tend to hide in dark confined spaces such as closets, under the bed or a piece of furniture, or in small crevices such as a crawl space in or under a building. Some may run into a forest and seek out dark caves, thick poorly accessible overgrown areas, possibly even a water source such as a pond or lake. Why? It is because the instinctual response for a person with autism is eliminating any stimulation because of an overload, whether cognitive or sensory. Being so overly stimulated, any further outside stimulation in any form increases the stress level, requiring an overworked brain to interpret and process the stimuli, which it cannot do. As a result the individual will seek out dark quiet places completely devoid of any stimulation to compensate for being overly stimulated. This too can be very dangerous. Because the individual is fleeing based purely on instinct they are unaware of their surroundings. Once in a place that allows them to calm down and cognitive functioning begins to return, they may become aware that they are in an unfamiliar spot. Not knowing their way back, panic sets in and a second meltdown could occur.

Witnessing self injurious behavior during a meltdown

Some autistics, particularly non verbal individuals, will resort to self injurious behavior such as head banging or biting themselves on the forearm and hand during a meltdown phase. Often it is a form of communication to express their level of frustration but sometimes it can be a diversion from one stressor to another. It could be done in an attempt to feel some sensory input while the brain is overloaded. Unfortunately because of the increasing pain threshold levels the gratification they seek cannot be registered so they intensify their self injurious behaviors. At one point they may be biting themselves but the instinctual mode of the brain interprets it as an attack from an outside source, responding with an intensifying of the biting as a defensive response.

It is really difficult to pinpoint the reasoning behind self injurious behavior so it is critical that if you have an individual who engages in such behavior to thoroughly investigate when, why, and how such behaviors became established. Generally speaking self injurious behavior is an extreme behavioral response to a stressor, seen more commonly in non verbal individuals as a way to communicate severe distress. Unfortunately such behaviors could be the result of underlying severe trauma from either physical or psychological sources. Sometimes these causes are not apparent. In my consulting work in this area I have found that self injurious behaviors in non verbal children often become ingrained due to well meaning but inappropriate interventions. It usually begins months or years earlier during an escalation period right before the actual meltdown. Keep in mind that all behaviors are a form of communication. As the child begins to escalate their behavior into physical manifestations such as thrashing, flailing limbs, or throwing themselves onto the ground someone tries to restrain them in hopes of either stopping the behavior or calming the individual down. This only increases their anxiety level so that they lash out by biting or head banging as a way to communicate frustration. This results in further restraint which in turn triggers an intense instinctual self preservation mode, decreasing cognitive functioning. At one point the biting or banging become an automatic response of the body which assumes it is being attacked.

It then becomes a vicious cycle where interveners attempt to stop such behaviors during a meltdown, only increasing the intensity of the self injurious behaviors. I have spoken to hundreds of caregivers and professionals who have tried to stop such behaviors in their non verbal client and they have unanimously confirmed that doing so only aggravated the situation and made the meltdown worse.

Can self injurious behaviors occur in the Asperger's population?

Head banging and even biting does occur in the high functioning and Asperger's population but not as frequently. This behavior is extremely difficult to diagnose as meltdown or tantrum and will require a working knowledge of how the individual handles stressors and frustrations in general. As a broad guideline the earlier the injurious behavior begins in an escalation phase the more likely it is a learned behavior designed to get attention. I will deal with this when discussing tantrums in Chapter 6. As long as they are cognitively aware of their surroundings then it isn't an instinctual response. That said, though, it doesn't mean that such behaviors are always a choice. Once the fight or flight response is triggered it can become an instinctual defense mechanism, albeit a faulty one. The same principle applies for verbal individuals as well as non verbal individuals: never restrain them during this time as it will only serve to increase those behaviors. The time to deal with such behaviors is when the person is cognitively fully functioning and not under stress.

The physiological response of the body during a meltdown

There is also a physiological component to the meltdown phase that must be understood before being able to effectively understand how to intervene during a meltdown. That important component is the effect of anxiety on the body which in turn triggers the fight or flight response. Preceding every meltdown or catastrophic reaction there is increasing anxiety which manifests itself in outward behaviors. This usually begins to occur when the autistic person's frustration level increases due to some stressors, such as being overstimulated, not getting an answer to a question they asked in a comprehendible way, or an abrupt change in plans or scripts. This creates anxiety which causes a rush of adrenaline to flood through the person's body and prepare them for the fight and flight response. If the anxiety isn't controlled by addressing or remedying the situation it will continue to build until it reaches a critical level that triggers the fight or flight response.

Nature designed our body with many failsafes. One such failsafe is in place during this fight or flight response. Well before the point where the brain switches from cognitive to instinctual functioning, the body naturally tries to release the amount of adrenaline by increasing physical activity as a way to "vent" or burn off the accumulating hormone, like a release valve. This venting always manifests itself in observable signs, particularly in an increase in stim behaviors. Every human being, autistic or not, will resort to this form of release when anxiety levels increase to a dramatic level. Increased breathing, clenching of fists, and foot tapping are commonly seen when non autistic people feel anxious or provoked into a fight response. Trying to forcibly stop the autistic individual engaging in such behaviors will only increase the anxiety and quickly develop into a meltdown. These behaviors are a warning sign of an impending meltdown. The best thing you can do is try to find out the cause of the sudden anxiety and deal with the root of the cause instead of becoming focused on the stim-like behaviors. I will deal with inappropriate stim behavior in Chapter 6, but for now it is important that you allow the person with autism that physical release through stimming. It is a natural coping mechanism we engage in that helps to calm us down. I engage in it frequently when stressed as a means to self regulate the increasing level of anxiety in a stressful situation.

Anxiety levels left unchecked will eventually lead to a meltdown. Look for warning signs of an impending fight or flight response. Cognitive functioning will decrease close to this point so behaviors such as pressured speech, incoherent sentences or thoughts, perseveration on a topic, echolalia, and difficulty understanding and answering questions will be common.

Common warning signs and behaviors indicating increasing anxiety, leading to a meltdown

- An increase in stimming such as quickened pacing, rocking, hand flapping.

- Echolalia (repeating the same word or sentence continually).

- Bursting out into singing or humming a tune repeatedly which increases in intensity.

- Difficulty understanding or answering questions.

- Perseverating on a favorite topic especially when in a stressful situation.

- Pressured loud speech.

- Fragmented and/or incoherent thoughts, sentences, and actions.

- Self endangerment by acting impulsively or recklessly.

- Getting in someone else's personal space and possibly even staring them in the eyes. I have witnessed this numerous times when individuals, in a desperate attempt to be understood, try to convey this by getting up close and personal as a means of having you take them very seriously and being able to see your expression.

- Any outward physical sign of anxiety such as leg shaking, hands trembling, nervous tics, spontaneous incoherent vocalizations, or behaviors resembling Tourette's Syndrome.

- Inability to recognize familiar people, places, objects, or special interests.

- The inability to be redirected back on task when accompanied by physical signs of stimming.

- Obsessing on the problem, adding "what if?" scenarios to all your possible solutions.

Of course there are endless possibilities of how each individual manifests physical signs of anxiety. I cannot stress enough how critical it is for you to know the person you are with. Find out in advance their behaviors or reactions to stressors and be on the lookout for them. Know also what coping mechanisms work for calming them down in advance.

The "freeze" response heralds an impending meltdown

If the anxiety is ignored and the problem not dealt with eventually or sometimes very suddenly and unexpectedly, it will progress to the next phase, the fight or flight response. Just before this response is triggered the brain has to completely switch from cognitive to instinctual functioning. This will occur during the "freeze" response. I have spent 24 years as a professional wildlife rehabilitator caring for injured or orphaned wild mammals and releasing them back into the wild when they are ready. Animals do have cognitive functioning but not as advanced as a human. They are mainly instinctual creatures and in my work with them as a rehabilitator I had to really become an expert in looking for signs of distress. An animal in a fight or flight response is very dangerous. Either they will attack you or attempt to run away; both are terrible scenarios for someone handling them. I learned to look for the "freeze" response which heralded either an attack on me or an attempt to run away. With some animals this response was dramatic and in others very subtle. I had to familiarize myself with each individual animal's behavioral patterns to be able to recognize the freeze response unique to that individual. If ever you surprise a feral cat wandering through your yard the first thing they do is freeze. Being frozen if only for a second allows the brain to activate the fight or flight response and choose which action best suits the circumstance. The same principle applies when you catch a deer in the headlights of your vehicle driving down a country road at night and it freezes, momentarily unable to move. This too is the initial phase of the fight or flight response.

Many pet owners accidently get bitten or seriously injured when trying to break up a fight between their pet and another animal. The pet has switched to a completely instinctual response and doesn't recognize its beloved owner. When it senses being touched it automatically perceives that touch as a threat and will attack as a means of self protection. This is very common in dog attacks where the master tries to break up the fighting animals only to be mauled by their own dog. When the dog has calmed down it doesn't remember the actual attack so it goes back to showing affection for its master.

The freeze response will be seen in autistic individuals just before the point of losing all cognitive abilities. It may be very blatant, like that of a startled animal, or very subtle like a faraway look in their eyes. The freeze response can vary in the same individual depending on the stressful circumstance.

Once while observing a young child with Asperger's during a teaching session I noticed that he was having difficulty understanding the lesson. The way in which the lesson was being taught was confusing even to me. At one point the teacher asked him to repeat what he just heard in his own words to assure her he comprehended the lesson. Immediately his face went blank and he had a far off stare. Attempts to get his attention failed. I began to see evidence of rapidly rising anxiety levels as his hands began flapping wildly. The teacher immediately began to get the nurse as this young man was diagnosed with a seizure disorder and this episode was a classic example of the type of seizures he had. He only had seizures during times of intense stress. Since I was familiar with his calming strategies I implemented them while waiting for the nurse to arrive. It took only a few short minutes to return the young boy to his normal state by utilizing his personal calming strategies as noted in his behavioral plan. The nurse was surprised that the seizure had abated so quickly because in the past he would have been down on the floor flailing his arms and crying uncontrollably. I have years of experience as an emergency medical technician where I worked for an ambulance company. Having been called to numerous epileptic seizures during that time I developed a trained eye to spot the various physical manifestations of a seizure. I knew instinctively in this situation that the boy was not experiencing a seizure based on the presenting symptoms but had a freeze response activated when the teacher caught him off guard and asked him to repeat back to her what she just said. Without the proper meltdown strategies to de-escalate the situation, he continued on the fight or flight response path with the result being a meltdown.

I am of course not saying that all autistic individuals diagnosed with seizure disorders are only having meltdowns. Such a diagnosis should be reserved for neurologists who have the expertise to evaluate a person for such a disorder. All I am saying is that a lot of autistic people are diagnosed with a seizure disorder and I can't help but question if some of them are only displaying a freeze response and not having a petit mal seizure, especially when they occur only during stressful times and can be halted through implementation of calming techniques. This is especially true in light of the fact that a seizure and meltdown have some "symptoms" in common. In a full blown meltdown there may be a blackout period where the person is totally unaware of his surroundings, what is going on, and who is there. In meltdowns where individuals are head banging they seem impervious to pain. After the meltdown they are usually physically and mentally exhausted, unable to concentrate for a while, and don't remember what just happened. These behavioral patterns are very similar to what is seen in a seizure.

Immediately after the highly excitable part of the meltdown phase

I must also stress that a critical period in the meltdown phase is immediately afterwards. As the person's cognitive functioning begins to return and they are becoming aware of their surroundings they can easily react in panic if the environment is unfamiliar. If the person is moved out of the area that they last remembered during a meltdown, it will completely disorientate them, perhaps setting off a panic attack which will start another meltdown phase. I have talked with a few school officials who told me their policy was to call the police or even an ambulance when an autistic student has a meltdown or to have them forcibly moved to the nurse's office in the school. Imagine how terrified autistic Timmy must feel to lastly remember being in math class and then "waking up" (becoming aware) in the nurse's office. The setting is unfamiliar, the people are unfamiliar, and it was not scripted. Most likely any conversation will focus on what just occurred, how the student behaved, and asking them why they melted down. Feeling physically and mentally drained, not to mention completely remorseful, it is almost impossible to get rational, concrete answers while harboring a feeling of disorientation during this post meltdown period. The stress of trying to discuss what just occurred may create such anxiety it escalates into another meltdown. It is very important for whoever is with an autistic individual during this time to offer reassurance and answers to any questions they may have in concrete well defined language.

Summary: phases of a cognitive meltdown

1. Frustration and/or confusion over a miscommunication, task, or assignment.

2. Rising anxiety levels with outward physical manifestations.

3. Perseverating or obsessing over the issue at hand with inability to process rational solutions offered.

4. Dramatically increased anxiety with irrational behaviors.

5. A freeze response anywhere from blatantly noticeable to barely visible lasting only seconds.

6. Fight or flight response triggered with either an urgency to run away from the situation or crying, wailing, flailing limbs with combative behavior if touched. Some individuals may have a "shut down" at this point, meaning they completely disengage from any form of communication. They appear "lost" in their own world and are unable to be refocused back to the moment.

7. Initial post meltdown feelings of remorse accompanied by physical and mental exhaustion.

8. Ingrained fear of it happening again under similar circumstances. If not dealt with properly this will lead to avoidance of any activity that the individual associates with that particular meltdown.

One of the aftermaths of a meltdown, which happens because it was so traumatic that the individual fears any repeat, is that they will avoid engaging in future activities or conversations that triggered the last meltdown. It is crucial that perhaps a day or two later someone sits down with the autistic individual when everyone is calm, and systematically discusses what happened, not in a confrontational tone but in an affirmative objective tone with the goal of looking at ways to prevent such a meltdown in the future.

SENSORY MELTDOWNS

Sensory meltdowns follow the same pattern as a cognitive meltdown but occur for different reasons. Many on the autism spectrum have some degree of sensory integration difficulties along with heightened senses, which creates sensory overloads in certain environments. Being in a physical environment that continuously bombards a sense or senses without any means of reducing that overstimulation will have the same effect as a cognitive overload. At some point the body cannot tolerate that sensation anymore and a sensory meltdown occurs.

Sensory overstimulation is unbearable. Here are a few examples where non autistic individuals would experience a similar feeling of sensory overload. It will give you an idea of the frustration levels autistic people experience in settings with sensory overstimulation.

If you are a dog or cat owner and have ever gotten a pet hair in your mouth, you are familiar with how intensely frustrating it becomes when your tongue keeps rolling it around all inside your mouth without being able to pinpoint exactly its spot for removal. The more your tongue tries to corner it the more it feels like a million hairs in your mouth. Drinking a glass of water doesn't relieve the sensation that it is still clinging to the back of your tongue.

Being awakened at night by the constant droning sound of a mosquito buzzing in your ears is a form of sensory overload. After a while you end up swatting the air in anticipation of another buzz even if the insect isn't within earshot. Inaudible a few feet away, when the mosquito is only inches away from your ear it has the roar of a speeding freight train. I wonder how many countless innocent sleeping partners besides my husband fall victim to the irrational behaviors of a person experiencing mosquito induced sensory overload. Eventually, after enduring the noise for so long and unable to sleep through it, the mosquito has you crazed and bent on killing it. It finally perches on your peacefully sleeping spouse's forehead taunting you to swat it which of course you do without any forethought of the ramifications of your actions. Your spouse wakes abruptly and demands an explanation of such an unprovoked slap and the only rational explanation is that the mosquito was driving you so crazy you couldn't tolerate it any more.

Walking with a pebble in your shoe will by no means physically cripple a person, yet most people do not tolerate that sensation for too long without stopping to remove the shoe and offending pebble.

Every human being has some degree of sensory limitations in one area or another. If overpowering perfumes make you nauseous your body is reacting to a sensory overload whether you are aware of it or not. Having a small piece of hay stuck in your sock rubbing against your skin or a tree leaf falling down the back of your shirt can be of no consequence to some but maddening to others. Imagine these same scenarios with senses heightened tenfold? To a child with autism something as benign to you as a clothing tag rubbing against the back of the neck feels like coarse sandpaper grating away the skin.

The sensory nightmares are endless so again I urge you to understand the autistic individual you are around. Find out their sensory issues and be mindful of the environment that may trigger an overload. Take pre-emptive action, such as removing the individual from the environment or reducing the intensity of the stimulating factor. If you have a child who cannot tolerate being touched then don't take that child to a crowded movie theater to see a film on opening day or during peak show times. Under those circumstances it is a given that there will be accidental brushing up by someone while waiting in line, or even getting bumped while seated when someone tries to exit the row.

How a sensory meltdown differs from a cognitive one

Unlike cognitive meltdowns sensory meltdowns are more of a chain reaction of physical sensations that doesn't respond to rational explanation but to the cessation of the offending stimulus. It is the body more than the mind reacting to outside stressors. I have in the past attempted to deal with an impending sensory overload by trying to convince myself it wasn't as bad as I was making it out to be and that I could endure it. I even rationally explained to myself that something as trivial as an annoying clothing tag on my neck isn't a catastrophe in the making. After all clothing manufacturers would not keep on putting clothing tags on the back of shirts if it was a sensory nightmare to consumers. I have never heard of a public outcry for the demand to stop clothing tags being sewn on the necks of shirts and tops. Therefore I tried to convince myself I was just overreacting. Despite the logical rationalization my body overrode my mind and eventually I ended up running into the bedroom disrobing as I went with scissors in hand to cut off the tags.

Accepting sensory limits

Desensitization through a process of gradually and incrementally getting an individual to endure a particular stressor has to be used with caution in sensory cases. While many fine techniques exist to help in the area of sensory integration there will be certain limits where a person cannot desensitize to a particularly stressful sensory trigger. I have encountered many well meaning parents insisting their autistic child just "grin and bear it" through a lengthy shopping adventure full of powerful sensory triggers because they so desperately craved for their child to be normal. When I ask how it went the usual response is "terribly," hence why they have sought my help. Sometimes it will require complete avoidance. I personally cannot tolerate the sensory issues associated with large crowded gatherings so I do not attend rock concerts, crowded country festivals and fairs, or shopping malls during peak Christmas shopping hours. I know my limits and have developed plans to work around them which allows me to avoid sensory triggers yet doesn't prevent me from interacting with the world around me.

The most valuable asset in coming up with a plan to minimize sensory meltdowns is to incorporate an occupational therapist in the process of developing a crisis plan to handle such emergencies. They are trained professionals with a virtual cornucopia of tools and skills designed to satisfy sensory cravings and effectively deal with sensory meltdowns. In sensory meltdowns it is critical to identify which sensory triggers elicited the meltdown and try to reduce or eliminate the offender. This is their area of specialty where they can be equally as effective with adults as children in dealing with nightmarish sensory issues.

If a sensory trigger becomes too overpowering the autistic individual may resort to self illuminating the stressor by any means possible. This is where a child with sensory issues revolving around clothing will start taking clothes off regardless of where they are if the sensations become too great to handle. The child with auditory issues will yell for everyone at a party to shut up if overstimulated by the sound of talking. They may resort to desperate inappropriate measures to eliminate the sensory triggers. When you attempt to restrain them from doing so they may become combative if you are too close and in their personal space.

Summary: sensory meltdowns

- Sensory meltdowns are an involuntary response to prolonged exposure to a sensory trigger.

- Differ from a cognitive meltdown because it is the body and not the mind that becomes overly stimulated.

- Once in the full meltdown phase the interventions for cognitive and sensory meltdowns are identical.

- During the meltdown phase they will display very similar behaviors to those seen in cognitive meltdowns.

- There will be a tendency towards aggressive, combative, or self injurious behavior if someone attempts to stop the individual from reducing the offending stimuli.

- The use of stim tools to calm or ease the stress of an offending sensory trigger is highly effective if utilized before the freeze, fight or flight response.

Cognitive and sensory meltdowns
SHUT DOWN RESPONSES: THE OTHER EXTREME OF A MELTDOWN PHASE

Not every individual will experience full blown outwardly visible meltdowns. There is a segment of the autism population that instead disengage because the added burden of interpreting communication or accepting commands is too taxing on an already overly stressed brain. These individuals will become very quiet and seem to retreat into their own personal world. They will not respond to verbal commands but they are still experiencing the same phases of a meltdown complete with the fight or flight response. If you try to force them to communicate by touching them, they too will instinctively lash out in a self preservation mode. These children will often sit in a corner on the floor, humming or just engaging in repetitive stim behaviors, oblivious to their surroundings. Being a meltdown that is directed inward they don't display the dramatic behaviors seen in other meltdowns and consequently may be misinterpreted as an act of defiance or refusal to stay on task. Because of the complete disengagement these meltdowns are much harder to manage because you are unable to properly assess what the individual is feeling and what interventions are working in restoring a sense of calm during the shut down phase. Remember, they disengage because of cognitive or sensory overload. Attempting to force communication in this state only serves to further deeply withdraw the individual from the environment around them. Earlier in this chapter I talked about thinking of an individual shutting down as a computer needing to be turned off when it freezes. Try to refrain from placing more cognitive demands on an already overloaded brain. Allow them a chance to "reboot" by giving them some "down" time where they can focus internally on alleviating the stressful situation through self stimming. There is little differentiation between a shut down as part of a meltdown and a shut down tantrum as a result of not wanting to be compliant. You will have to really familiarize yourself with the autistic individual's triggers and responses to such triggers to know the difference.

THE AFTERMATH OF A MELTDOWN: INTENSE FEELINGS OF REMORSE, EMBARRASSMENT, AND SHAME

Once the adrenaline has been expended the body naturally but slowly transitions from instinctual mode back to pre-meltdown cognitive functioning. The individual may be unaware of what just transpired but be full of remorse, guilt, and shame for having had such a public display of inappropriate behaviors. Fears of abandonment because of it will be prevalent. They may ask constantly, "Do you still love me?" "Are you still my friend?" "Will you still see me?"

They may ask meekly if they have lost a certain privilege or outing because of their behavior. Some may be fearful to return to the place where the meltdown occurred because of fears of ridicule or rejection by those who witnessed it, especially peers. As an act of contrition they may be overly compliant because of inner feelings of guilt and shame and are extremely vulnerable during this time to impulsively agree to conditions that aren't in their best interest. Once during my employment with a company I had a foreseeable meltdown due to not having reasonable accommodations in place to offset the sensory triggers of the environment I was forced to work in, despite my prior voiced concerns over the issue. Despite all attempts to avoid a meltdown, it did occur, and I was so remorseful afterwards my boss drew up a contract for me to sign right there and then stating that if I had a another meltdown I would accept the consequence of being terminated for it. It was a complete violation of my rights but the intense guilt of not being able to stop a meltdown clouded my judgment so I signed the document. Eventually another meltdown happened due to their unwillingness to offer a reasonable accommodation so I quit before having to endure the added shame of being fired for something beyond my control.

The post meltdown period will have many individuals agreeing to do things just to redeem themselves in the eyes of the people who witnessed the meltdown. They are vulnerable and at risk for being taken advantage of during this time. They need affirmation not condemnation.

Chapter 6

How Does a Tantrum Differ from a Meltdown?

A meltdown or catastrophic episode is an involuntary reaction due to cognitive overload or sensory overstimulation. It isn't a conscious choice or ploy for attention, but rather an unfortunate series of behaviors that unfolds at times rather rapidly and at other times builds up gradually due to prolonged exposure to stressors. Meltdowns aren't a planned event where we have to meet a certain quota of meltdowns per day. They happen at the worst possible times despite our best attempts to self regulate. Meltdowns unleash a physiological autonomic bodily response to overwhelming stressors that can impart herculean strength to the smallest of statures during a fight or flight response. I have designed specific intervention strategies that deal with de-escalating a meltdown or at least minimizing the impact that are very successful when implemented correctly. I have outlined these strategies in Chapter 9.

In a nutshell, when you are trying to contain the situation in a meltdown you are dealing with someone who isn't thinking but acting on pure instinct. It can be a very dangerous time, with harm inflicted on the intervener if they happen to get too close.

Thankfully aggression is limited to violations of personal space and then even the individual is unaware who they are lashing out at. Aggression is *never* targeted towards a specific person who is out of arm's length. In other words, if you stand back about five feet from the person having a meltdown you should not be in danger of getting hit, bitten, or kicked.

Tantrums on the other hand are conscious voluntary choices to manipulate another individual through behaviors in order to achieve a desired result. Not only are tantrums planned but individuals are targeted based on their vulnerability to give in to these demands. Non verbal children are just as clever as high functioning children when it comes to knowing who to manipulate through a tantrum. By far the bulk of my consulting services revolves around distinguishing when a client is having a meltdown and when it is just a tantrum, and teaching staff the proper interventions for both. It is crucial to understand that meltdown interventions are polar opposites of tantrum interventions, so one must be very precise in establishing which of the two is occurring. They can appear nearly identical at times.

To truly pinpoint whether the individual is melting down or just behaving badly one must understand how the autistic mind processes anxiety. The first four chapters of this book covered the fundamentals of understanding how we handle stressors. If you haven't already read the preceding chapters I strongly recommend that you go back and do so before continuing with this chapter because without that understanding it will be nearly impossible for you to differentiate whether the individual is responding to overwhelming stress or merely acting out.

The golden rule in meltdowns and tantrums

No matter what interventions or strategies you feel are appropriate the golden rule in dealing with meltdowns and tantrums is consistency. The behavioral plan established and agreed upon for a particular student or adult must be followed to the letter at home as well as at school and vice versa. Most behavioral issues and tantrums result from a break in that consistency. Children are children whether they have autism or not and will probe for "weak spots" by testing the limits or boundaries imposed upon them by parents, caregivers, professionals, and teachers. It doesn't make them a bad child, just a typical one. I have had countless teachers approach me after my meltdown training complaining that in their hearts they know a particular autistic student is tantruming and not melting down but the parents keep insisting it is a meltdown and use autism as an excuse for such behavior. I have also had numerous parents complain to me that their autistic child has meltdowns and they can pinpoint the stressors at school but the school insists the child is tantruming for attention and refuses to offer reasonable accommodations that would reduce the number of meltdowns the child is having. Generally the problem revolves around not understanding how that particular student handles stressors. I cannot overstress how important and crucial it is for everyone who is working with an autistic child to remember to be consistent in everything, including behavioral plans and consequences for bad behavior.

I remember one incident when I was a child where I was tantruming and my mother, who had no idea I was autistic, handled the situation in the only way she knew would be effective. She set the limit and then refused to back down no matter what. I was about seven years old. For dinner my mother served Brussels sprouts as the vegetable with the meal. I honestly don't remember exactly what prompted my refusal to eat them but I believe it was because I was in a hurry to leave the dinner table and go outside to play in the garden. It had nothing to do with sensory concerns or some other component of autism, I just felt non compliant and decided to stand my ground and not eat them. The response from my mother was very typical of the times; if I didn't eat them I would get nothing else till I did. That meant I would forfeit dessert too. I didn't care as I was full anyway. My mother decided that she didn't want to listen to my complaints any longer during dinner so I was dismissed and allowed to go out and play. I thought I had scored a great victory because my being fussy and irritable got me excused from the dinner table without having to eat the Brussels sprouts. My mother never raised her voice or even brought up the fact that I was acting inappropriately at the dinner table for a young lady. I thought for sure she would forget about the whole incident by morning.

When morning came and it was time for breakfast my mother's behavior was no different from any other morning and I was looking forward to a pleasant meal before school. Then she served me on my breakfast plate six wrinkled Brussels spouts, the very same ones I refused to eat at dinner. She reminded me in a calm voice that I would get nothing else to eat till I ate them. Indignant at her actions I staunchly refused to eat even one saying I preferred to starve to death. Of course I got the lecture about all the starving children in third world countries who would be grateful for six wrinkled Brussels sprouts to eat. I crossed my arms in defiance and told her to send the sprouts to them in a care package. She didn't react but just stayed very calm and collected, and ignored my comment. What I wasn't aware of was that my mother had called my teacher at school apprising her of the situation. She asked her to stay firm in her resolve to not back down should I offer up some very heartfelt pleas for food during the school day. My mother was determined to teach me a lesson that she would not be held hostage by my tantrums.

I went off to school feeling hungry yet still stubborn in my refusal to be compliant regarding eating the sprouts. Surely my mother would give in by now and in my lunch pail I would find a tasty sandwich. I did have a back up plan just in case I was wrong and my sandwich turned out to be Brussels sprouts. I was confident that at school during lunch if I looked really pitiful the teacher would have mercy upon me and offer me something to eat of hers. (Back then we didn't have a cafeteria or hot lunches but had to pack our own in brown bags or lunch pails.) When it was time for lunch I discovered six wrinkly, shriveled up Brussels sprouts neatly packaged in my lunch pail. To be truthful I was so shocked that to this day I remember every detail as if it happened only yesterday. It was time for plan B, which was to guilt the teacher into overriding my mother's actions by playing up the fact of how cruel it was to send a young child to school with such a non nutritious and disgusting looking lunch. I had counted on my sad puppy dog expression to tug at her heart strings and manipulate her into giving me something tasty to eat. Imagine my surprise when the teacher told me quite firmly that if I didn't eat my Brussels sprouts for lunch I wouldn't get anything else to eat, just like my mother said. I asked her how she knew my mother's intentions and I got the old "a little birdie flew in and told me" answer. At that point I realized my mother wasn't going to back down and now she had the teacher on her side. Who else would she solicit to help her and how long did she plan on continuing? I decided right there and then that no matter what I did I wasn't going to get my way of not eating the sprouts so I ate them for lunch. They actually tasted really good, considering I was hungry by then, and to this day I love Brussels sprouts. When I got home my mom already knew I ate them and never mentioned the incident again nor did I ever challenge her again at meal times.

The point of this story was that I was trying to manipulate my mother by behaving badly. She didn't reinforce this behavior by arguing with me. My mother stayed the course once she decided to set the limit and the key here is consistency. She knew if she was to be successful in this matter she would have to have others who had an influence over my meal times in on her plan. What she implemented at home ended up being implemented at school. It didn't take me long to realize that tantruming wouldn't achieve the desired result. Granted this incident was rather mild in terms of outward behaviors. I wasn't screaming or throwing things but it was the first time I decided to challenge my mother. Had my mother not been firm and consistent it would have set a precedent, with me trying it again in the future to get my way knowing she would eventually back down. It could easily have become a learned bad behavior that day but it didn't. Consistency and staying firm as a figure of authority is what I ended up respecting. My behaviors were not a result of autism but of defiance.

Tantrums are a choice

Unlike meltdowns tantrums are a learned response. Tantrums if rewarded will only increase in intensity and frequency over time. Once such behavior is established it will take patience, firmness, and time to correct such ingrained manipulative actions. Unchecked tantrums can escalate into aggressive behaviors towards others where the individual actually targets a specific person and then consciously decides to physically assault them. In a tantrum there is no cognitive dysfunction and complete awareness of their surroundings. I have created a checklist of the distinguishing features of meltdowns and tantrums. Use this as a guide to help in determining whether an individual is having a meltdown or just tantruming. However, use caution as this is merely a guide of general characteristics. In order to correctly utilize the appropriate interventions, know your child's or client's behavioral patterns, triggers, and responses to anxiety. Meltdown interventions as well as tantrum strategies must be tailored to each individual.

Distinguishing a meltdown from a tantrum: a checklist

1. Meltdowns always involve a level of cognitive dysfunction, tantrums do not.

2. Meltdowns are an unconscious reaction to either cognitive or sensory overload. Tantrums are a conscious deliberate choice to behave a certain way to manipulate others.

3. In a meltdown there will be an increase in intensity of stimming behaviors and physical manifestations of uncontrollable anxiety. In a tantrum there may be outward physical movements such as kicking, screaming, flailing arms but they are controlled movements that are easily altered to achieve a desired reaction.

4. The explosiveness of a meltdown is due to too much adrenaline (stress hormone) built up in the body which is then released quickly through physical means. It will be time limited as once the hormone depletes itself the body returns to its pre-meltdown state. Usual time is 20–40 minutes but may vary a little. In a tantrum the explosiveness can last hours if not even days and adrenaline only rises to meet the needs of the actions of the intended behavior.

5. Because of the adrenaline reaching critical levels, once a meltdown has reached the fight or flight response it cannot be stopped due to the engagement of the instinctual fight and flight mechanism. A tantrum can stop instantly at any time or be intermittent because it is never a result of a fight or flight response.

6. Meltdowns have specific triggers related to stressors; tantrums are acts of defiance over an issue.

7. Bargaining is never a component of a meltdown but a tactic employed in tantrums to probe weaknesses in set boundaries, i.e. "I don't want to eat all my Brussels sprouts but how about if I eat just one?"

8. Unfortunately a tantrum can develop into a meltdown if the individual gets extremely worked up, but a meltdown can *never* turn into a tantrum.

9. There will be post meltdown feelings of shame, guilt, humiliation, and remorse over how their behavior was perceived and witnessed by those around them. In a tantrum there is either a sense of satisfaction for achieving the desired response, or frustration and some level of anger over not being successful in manipulating others.

10. After the meltdown is over the individual is physically and mentally exhausted and may have limited awareness, if any, of what just transpired. In a tantrum the individual has excellent recall of the episode with little or no physical exhaustion.

11. In escalating anxiety heading towards a meltdown the individual will have a tendency towards not wanting to talk or go in depth into a conversation with someone else, or even discuss what is causing such a response because the brain is already cognitively overtaxed and limited in its processing abilities. In a tantrum the behaviors are attention seeking, wanting the maximum impact occurring while around others.

12. Aggressive behavior in a meltdown is never targeted against a specific individual, but an instinctual response of self preservation if someone comes within their personal space boundary. In tantrums it is very common to direct aggression against either an innocent bystander or the person setting the limits.

Controlling established tantrums

Established tantrums are very difficult to control because they are directly proportionate to how successful they have been in the past. Tantrums start out first as an act of defiance. If successful the individual continues that behavioral response, first in future identical situations and then in other situations. When someone along the way decides not to back down from a demand, this not only surprises the individual who has gotten away with it to that point but also angers them, so they begin to escalate their behaviors to overpower the person staying firm in their resolve not to give in. This is why when an intervention is first implemented the offending behaviors increase dramatically, in hopes of frightening or bullying you to back down and let them have their own way. This is an extremely dangerous crossroad as at times these individuals will resort to physical violence to create fear and gain control. They empower themselves by taking away your power through the threat of physical retaliation against another individual, such as a classmate sitting next to them or even you should you pursue the matter. Unchecked physical acts of aggression on another will only escalate over time if not stopped, especially in young males.

I have had parents come up to me terrified of their teenage autistic son when he is angry because he can literally throw them across the room. They want to know how to handle his explosive rages towards them. As I ask a series of questions regarding how, when, why, and what was done the first time their child physically assaulted someone I find out every time that this behavior started years earlier as an act that went unpunished. Granted, it wasn't their child throwing them across a room, but it was him slapping or kicking his parents, siblings, or pets when he was told "no." As it was considered "harmless" the hitting or physical aggression part of the tantrum was never singled out and handled immediately. I have heard a list of reasons why such behavior was allowed to continue but that is of no use in dealing with the rage-filled situation at hand. Sadly if left unchecked this type of aggressive behavior will continue to escalate until intervention is required by police authorities. The younger the child displays such behavior the more critical it is to extinguish that type of aggression immediately. This goes for non verbal as well as verbal children. Physical aggressive behavior directed towards another is established through being rewarded by not incurring punitive measures for it.

How to handle a tantrum

The best interventions for tantrums are consequences (punishment) for inappropriate behaviors to teach a lesson. That lesson being that acting inappropriately never results in a desired reward and one must respect and obey authority, period. No discussion, no bargaining, no compromises. For every action there is a reaction, good or bad. The consequences must have an impact felt by the individual, and more importantly must be conveyed as being the direct result of behaving a certain way. The tantruming individual must make a connection between the particular behaviors and the consequences implemented so they learn this is the reaction to their action. If little Johnny becomes argumentative over not wanting to do homework when it is time to do so, don't simply say, "Go to your room." That doesn't explain why he is being sent. Is it for his intention of not doing homework or for being argumentative with his parent?

A better response would be, "Go to your room for raising your voice with me." This way there is a connection between the behavior and the consequence.

Try to make the punishment immediate, so its impact will be a direct reflection of the degree of misbehavior. Avoid instituting a punishment that will take effect in the future such as, "Because you misbehaved, you will not be able to go to the playground tomorrow." That conveys a subconscious message that they got away with it. After the tantrum has ended with the child behaving well the rest of the afternoon, it will be hard for them to make the connection of just why he or she lost playground privileges for the following day. I almost hate to use the analogy due to fear of being misinterpreted, but think along the lines of puppy training. A puppy is immediately reprimanded for an offending behavior so as to associate the reprimand with that particular behavior. If you have a dog that you catch in the act of chewing a slipper, you don't wait hours before scolding the dog for the offense because they won't make the connection that the punishment was for something that took place hours earlier. The same applies to children or even adults.

Equally important, one must ignore the offending behavior if possible. A behavior is done to get a reaction, any reaction including a negative one, so by ignoring it you aren't acknowledging that they have your undivided attention. It never ceases to amaze me how children and adults know exactly what to say to obtain a reaction of shock from us. They will prey on your fears knowing it is a weak spot. One of the biggest natural fears many parents have is of not being a good parent. When little Johnny screams at you in a defiant tone, "I hate you, you are a bad mommy," he rarely means it but uses that expression as a means to manipulate you through guilt. Knowing it is one of your fears he tries to manipulate you with it. If you react he knows this tactic is effective and then will be quick to build upon it. You will find yourself being held hostage by his demands. Autism is never an excuse for misbehaving. Treat the autistic child just like any other child in that situation.

A WORD OF CAUTION

I must also stress a warning regarding getting an individual to venture outside of their comfort zone. Sometimes they will balk and become very defiant at the mere thought of doing or trying something new or different, especially if it involves a change in routine. At times their reluctance may be interpreted as an act of defiance when in actuality it is due to unpredictability and the fear of the unknown. If this reluctance is accompanied by increasing anxiety it means that they need more scripting out or details with concrete timeframes in order to create a working script in their head. They may have no "visual" in their mind of what to expect. This is very distressing to them. They are *not* tantruming in this case but becoming anxious due to experiencing the unfamiliar. In a tantrum there will be no cognitive impairment. Their energy will be focused on getting you to give in to their demands. Again I am giving you very broad guidelines so it is imperative that you know the individual you are working or living with. Learn their behavioral responses to stressors as well as how they act when misbehaving.

There will be many times when just ignoring the bad behavior is either too dangerous or ineffective for the circumstance at that moment. A classic example of an ineffective strategy most of us have experienced involves the grocery store. It's the mother verses the child over wanting a candy bar and not getting it scenario. It usually resolves one of two ways. The child starts screaming and throwing themselves on the ground, especially in front of other customers. The mother, becoming embarrassed, begins to reason and even plead with their child to stop. The parent may try to compromise by offering them candy later on. Compromising is interpreted as begging by the tantruming child and is taken as a sign that the mother could be easily bullied into giving in to their demand. This usually escalates the tantrum because the child doesn't want it later but wants it now. Finally out of desperation and embarrassment the mother succumbs to this inappropriate display and hands the child the very candy she said "no" to earlier just so as to end the screaming and fussing. By trying to reason with the child she actually reinforced the bad behavior. The child will now utilize this effective means of self gratification in the future.

The second way this scenario can resolve itself is the best and most effective way of handling a tantrum. The child starts screaming demanding candy and flops to the ground in a most dramatic fashion. The mother calmly says, "Mary, if you don't stop screaming right now, you and I will leave our shopping cart where it stands and you and I are going to the car until you quiet down." The child continues screaming and crying so the mother takes the child by the hand and immediately walks out of the store towards the vehicle. Of course the child screams even louder because she knows her behavior isn't getting the attention she thought. The mother repeats to her daughter a few times as they are leaving, "Unless you quiet down we are not going to return to this store today."

Whenever I see a mother stand by her words I go up to her and affirm her for doing the right thing behavior wise. She is, after all, extremely embarrassed by this tantrum. After encouraging words from me the mother always feels validated and a sense that she isn't being judged by other customers as a cruel mother. In this second scenario the mother didn't get caught up in the drama but dealt with the tantrum by instituting an immediate consequence for the inappropriate behavior. She gave a clear message that inappropriate behavior will not be rewarded but will incur a consequence.

AGGRESSIVE OR SELF INJURIOUS BEHAVIOR DURING A TANTRUM

A much more difficult situation is a child who is self injurious or physically aggressive towards others during a tantrum. This is almost impossible to correctly handle in any setting because more than ever it will require that everyone in that individual's life be consistent in handling this type of behavior. Under normal circumstances ignoring the bad behavior is the most effective tool in curbing a tantrum, however, if the child or adult begins to bang their head into the nearest wall, or attack another student or teacher such bad behavior *must never* be ignored. Why? Because the tantruming child or adult will, if not getting a reaction, increase the intensity of the aggressive and/or self injurious behavior, resulting in possible injury to themselves or others. This is a most difficult situation to handle in the school. The first time such a tantrum is witnessed swift action is paramount. First attempt to minimize the impact of the hurtful behavior by either getting everyone out of the room (for their own safety) and/or placing something between the individual and the body part being injured to cushion the self inflicted blows. If during this attempt to protect the individual from self inflicting wounds, the individual attempts to bite, kick, or head bang you, you must immediately back away otherwise they *will* attack you. In this case there is not much else you can do, short of restraining the individual to the point they can't move. I am not a big supporter of this intense restraint but there may be times when it is either that or watch helplessly as a child or adult seriously injures themselves. All the while keep conversation with the individual to a minimum with firm statements explaining consequences that will be enacted if the behavior continues.

This tantrum will be a judgment call as to whether it is safe to simply watch the tantrum and not act, or intervene to prevent personal injury. Have someone call the parents, if available, or if you are alone wait till immediately after the tantrum and then call the parent yourself if you don't have a pre-established behavioral plan for aggressive behavior. Stress how this tantrum is dangerous to more than just the child and ask what concrete behavioral plan has been developed for this child to deal with such behaviors. If the parent says they have no such plan tell them the urgency of this situation requires a parent teacher and or team meeting to devise a behavioral plan to handle this type of intensity in a tantrum. It is to be hoped that the parent will agree to a meeting to come up with an effective plan to curb such behavior. If, however, the parent begins to make excuses or feels the situation isn't as critical as you have explained, your options are extremely limited. The only effective tool now is to not allow the child to return to school or the setting until a parent conference has been held. I know this seems harsh and impractical but unless you then set the boundary of zero tolerance for aggressive behavior neither the child nor parent will comprehend the significance of such inappropriate behavior. I cannot stress enough that if aggressive behavior has successfully resulted in the desired manipulated response such behavior will be repeated again and again, increasing in intensity, with the potential for severe injury to themselves and others over time.

INTERVENING SUCCESSFULLY

If there is a working behavioral plan on file for this child, use it. It is best to request assistance at this time from other school professionals who work with this child, to be there not only as a witness but also to intervene if they become more violently aggressive than you can handle. Have these individuals observe and take notes of the behaviors witnessed and what interventions were implemented successfully or unsuccessfully, preferably out of view of the child so as not to encourage them to escalate the violence. Remember they want an audience so keep interaction and onlookers to a bare minimum, but you need back up in case things get beyond the point where you can handle them alone, so it is imperative to have professionals on "stand by." In the heat of the moment dealing with an out of control individual you cannot concentrate on all the things going on around you. By having others take notes of the situation, afterwards during the incident review phase, observations that you may have missed might be crucial in revising the behavioral plan. These notes will be of great benefit by providing first hand accounts of what was happening in detail. The details will reveal much of what is missed in general mental recall of the incident.

A key point to remember in aggressive behaviors is that is done for attention and out of manipulation. If you react emotionally by getting upset, raising your voice, pleading with them to stop, or try to bargain with them it reinforces to them that they have you where they want. You *must* have an almost monotone voice that is steady, calm, and unwavering when issuing commands to stop. They must be commands and not requests or pleas to stop. No reasoning during the aggressive phase either. Simply repeat a few times throughout the tantrum the consequence they will incur for that behavior if they don't stop. Keep all communication to a bare minimum so as not to encourage the individual that they are successfully playing with your emotions.

Do not allow them to come up to you to physically assault you! If an individual begins to direct their aggression towards you, get out of the way. Walk behind a desk, step aside, and never stand close to them where they are within arm's reach. If the person is throwing objects it is unwise to attempt to remove all objects from their grasp as they will interpret that as a challenge and only increase their pace of grabbing an object before you do. In this situation contain the individual in the room. Make sure all exits are secured, leave the room yourself, and stand behind a door with a glass window or somewhere you can monitor the situation without risk to your personal safety. This will probably frustrate the individual into escalating the aggression at first but if you do not react they will quickly notice that the behavior is not having the desired impact and lose interest or they eventually will tire themselves out physically.

Self aggressive behavior or aggressive behavior towards another individual in a tantrum is extremely volatile and must be dealt with immediately in order to extinguish the aggressive outbursts. Unchecked aggression will only increase over time to the point of becoming life threatening to themselves or others witnessing this type of outburst. Never accept excuses for aggressive behaviors. There must be zero tolerance for aggression in a tantrum.

HOW TO TEST FOR A TANTRUM IN THE VERBAL INDIVIDUAL

When trying to determine if someone is tantruming or having a meltdown always, always, remember to test for cognitive functioning. Cognitive functioning is your most powerful key in assessing which of the two it is. If the individual is verbal a simple cognitive functioning test would be simple questions you know they should know the answer to such as, "What is my name?" and "What class are you in now?" "What is your home address?" and "What day is this?"

Questions that aren't complex or confusing will indicate if the individual is experiencing cognitive overload. If the child or adult responds inappropriately, seems confused, or begins to stutter or perseverate on a word, sentence, or topic it is more than likely a meltdown. Ask these questions even if the autistic individual is in a screaming, limbs flailing mode. If the individual despite all the dramatic behavior can respond clearly and succinctly, chances are they are tantruming. Every meltdown involves some degree of cognitive dysfunction depending on how severely the person experiences meltdowns. Tantrums do not.

HOW TO TEST FOR A TANTRUM IN THE NON VERBAL INDIVIDUAL

The same principle applies to non verbal individuals when assessing tantrum verses meltdown except, as they are non verbal, give a command for a simple task you know they can perform flawlessly. For instance Mary is screaming and rocking violently in her chair but you are unsure whether it is a tantrum or a meltdown. Mary is very competent to take a drink of water from her water glass in front of her. In a calm but firm voice say, "Mary, please take a drink of water from your water glass right now." If Mary tries to, but reaches instead for the pencil or fumbles handling the glass it is a good indicator that she is experiencing cognitive overload leading to a meltdown. If Mary refuses to follow your command but you know she heard every word look for outward signs of defiance. These children are really bad at hiding what they are feeling and if you are familiar with Mary's overall behavioral patterns then you will be able to ascertain whether it is a meltdown or tantrum. Don't forget every behavior is a form of communication. Non verbal children are very good at communicating how they are feeling just by their body language.

UTILIZING SPECIAL INTERESTS AND/OR OBJECTS TO TEST FOR A TANTRUM

Another good test for overall cognitive functioning to distinguish a meltdown from a tantrum involves utilizing special interests and favorite items. For the verbal child who seems to be spiraling ask them a question about their special interest that you know they would normally love to go into a monologue over. In my experience even a child tantruming seems to put the tantrum on hold in order to talk about their favorite special interest. If a child or adult, however, seems confused, forgets facts, or becomes frustrated at not having the normal exceptional recall of their favorite topic, more than likely they are experiencing the initial phases of an impending meltdown.

For the non verbal child or adult the same principle applies except we utilize their favorite stim tool or item. Let's say non verbal Mary is sitting in her chair screaming and fussing. You know she has a favorite stim tool, which is her teddy bear. It is the number one coping tool she clings to when distressed and she normally treats it like it was made of gold. She would never think of mishandling that stuffed bear. You place her favorite stim tool in front of her and without hesitation she flings it to the ground, never giving it a second thought. You are probably thinking this is a conclusive sign that it is a tantrum, right? Well you would be wrong. Chances are it is a meltdown. Why? Because Mary under normal circumstances would never think of casting her favorite stim tool on the ground and the fact that she did means she wasn't cognitively aware of what was in front of her.

This test will work only with the ultimate favorite item an individual cherishes. Trust me, I have seen non verbal individuals throw all sorts of things placed in front of them in hopes of appeasement, but when it came to their special favorite object they always managed to spare that item the careless toss to the ground. Such cognition indicates that they are not experiencing any processing difficulties one would expect to find in a meltdown situation.

LOOK FOR THE TELL TALE SIGNS OF ANXIETY

Once you have established cognitive function or dysfunction, look for another definitive sign that verifies your findings. Observe the outward signs of anxiety. This works best if you are familiar with how your autistic client, student, or child handles anxiety. While there is a lot of limb flailing and thrashing, in a tantrum it seems more controlled or regulated. The facial expression will be one of anger. The individual is in complete control of the physical movements and may suspend them momentarily for any reason. In a meltdown there will be intense stimming that doesn't stop or decrease spontaneously. The facial expression will be one of fear or panic.

NON SOCIAL TENDENCIES

Also at this point notice if they want to be left alone or are looking to engage you in communication. In a meltdown when cognitive functioning is taxed many autistic people will shy away from communicating with others because it is too demanding for an already overstressed brain. The whole point of a tantrum is to manipulate someone else into giving you want you want so obviously the individual will want to be around other people, otherwise there is no one to manipulate and the tantrum would be an exercise in futility.

I was once called in for a consultation regarding a young non verbal child who was having severe "meltdowns" according to his teacher and aides. His behaviors included throwing himself on the ground where he would scream and thrash so loudly it became a disruption to the students in other classrooms. Unfortunately the teacher and aides so feared his meltdowns they went out of their way to make sure he had whatever he wanted. His meltdowns revolved around learning new tasks. During this learning phase it was customary to use chocolate candies as a reward for completing one phase of the task and as an incentive to go onto the next part of the task. At some point "Timmy" wanted two pieces of chocolate instead of the usual one he received for successful completion. When the teacher said "no" the dramatic behaviors immediately commenced. The more they began to reason with him ("explain" was their term) why he couldn't have another piece the more intense his physical behaviors became. By now the teacher was in panic mode so she summoned the help of the school nurse, counselor, principal, and speech therapist. Little Timmy had an audience watching this display. Because Timmy is non verbal they assumed he was melting down because he did not understand the reason for not being allowed a second piece of candy. I actually had the pleasure of watching Timmy in action this particular day. All went as expected and I observed Timmy's body language and the reaction of those witnessing his "meltdown."

(Just a side note: while many autistic individuals lack the ability to read non verbal body language it seems this is limited to reading non autistic people's non verbal body language. I have found in all my experiences with fellow autistic individuals they are extremely accurate on reading non verbal body language in other autistic people. This also accounts for the unique and incredible bond many autistic individuals form with animals. Non verbal body language is an accurate portrayal of what we are feeling and it is honest. Animals and autistic individuals generally don't try to deceive others through body language or use vague non verbal gestures as a form of communication.)

After I observed Timmy for a few moments I asked the onlookers to please step out in the hallway and try not to peer intently at how Timmy was acting. I then went up to a screaming Timmy and firmly stated in a calm tone, "Timmy, I am not like your teachers so I am not going to acknowledge your tantrum. When you decide to calm down then I will communicate with you." As I was speaking Timmy immediately looked up at me when he heard his name called, indicating his cognitive functioning abilities were intact. Then I turned my back to him while he screamed and thrashed. What I noticed next was absolutely clever to my mind but I did not convey my thoughts to him. Timmy moved his tantrum into my peripheral visual field. He knew that I was autistic and assumed correctly that my peripheral vision was as sharp as his. As soon as he did this I said absolutely nothing and turned around so that I could not see him. It took only moments before he again moved his tantrum into my peripheral field, so I kept turning away. This continued for about 30 minutes until Timmy realized that I wasn't going to watch his behaviors or acknowledge them at all. Then this little non verbal boy completely stopped his thrashing around, stood up, and tugged at the side of my shirt ready and willing to continue on with the task he originally began.

It was very obvious that this young boy had manipulated those working with him into overreacting at his outbursts. In the end he was usually rewarded with two pieces of chocolate instead of the one that was part of his original plan for task completion. I explained to them that this was a classic tantrum and not a meltdown. We came up with a behavioral plan for when this happened again to do as I had done during my consultation. It was successful in the end at eliminating these outbursts though initially his behaviors escalated dramatically. However, the staff held firm and did not overreact to them and when Timmy realized this sort of behavior didn't solicit a reaction, he stopped. Whoever said non verbal children weren't smart?

INSTANT GRATIFICATION AS A POTENTIAL SOURCE OF TANTRUMS

I do want to caution those working with the non verbal population to avoid using instant gratification as a reward for either good behavior or step completion in task building. Instant gratifiers can be anything from food (candy, popcorn, fruit slices) to special objects, and toys that act as stim tools. Stim tools are the items that help calm down an individual who is becoming anxious and tend to be very specific. Stim tools should always be available to an individual who needs calming. For instance Timmy's stim tool is a little brightly multi-colored plastic car. That is what he stims on when feeling upset. Timmy is fascinated by any brightly colored object and will muse over them out of curiosity but the objects hold no special "power" when it comes to being an aid for anxiety. I have seen first hand what happens when a child earns a reward of being able to pick one object before moving on to the next phase of the task. The child is usually more interested in the object and will have trouble staying focused on task. When pressured to continue behaviors surface. Instant gratification will over time create a sense of entitlement.

USING A TOKEN SYSTEM AS AN EFFECTIVE ALTERNATIVE

A much more effective way of rewarding a child or adult is what I call the token system. Instead of immediately getting a reward for successful completion the individual earns a token for each phase of the task he completes correctly. At the end of the day they can "cash" them in for pre-designated items. These items as well as a representation of how many tokens it will take to "earn" them will be on a picture board as a visual aid and reminder throughout the day. Have you ever gone to a carnival, seen a booth with huge stuffed animals dangling from the ceiling and stopped at that booth to throw a dart at a balloon? The individual manning the booth entices you by saying every balloon has a guaranteed tag inside that corresponds with the level (size) of stuffed animal you could win. Up on the side of the booth there is a huge visual display that shows the different colored tags representing what prize category you can pick from. This token identification system allows the player upfront to know what the rewards could be if successful. Use this type of visual cue when setting up the rewards.

As I mentioned earlier, the same principle applies to us if we are in the workforce. If you go to work Monday through Friday and do what is expected in your job description then at the end of the work week you receive a piece of paper (token) which allows you to cash it in for money to buy what you want. It is much more effective than your employer handing you a few bags of groceries each week, isn't it? It teaches us patience (having to have to wait till payday), budgeting (in theory you can't be spending more than you earn, although many are doing it through credit cards and loans which isn't sound financially!), and work ethics because if you decide to not come in to work and not call in sick or take a vacation day then you get docked (lose) that day's wages. In the same way it teaches individuals that they are responsible for their actions which if appropriate will result in a reward. By allowing them to choose the reward it empowers them to make decisions and cognitively process which reward they desire the most. It teaches choice selection.

This token system is almost universal and can be applied to verbal and high functioning children and adults when trying to keep them on task. If you have a mainstreamed teenage student who is high functioning but prefers to play with his or her smart phone with all the apps as opposed to staying focused and paying attention in class, this token principle can be applied in similar terms. Just set up the ground rules: "Johnny, you cannot use your phone during class time. If you stay focused and committed to paying attention you can earn five minutes of game time on your smart phone at the end of the class lesson. You will have this same opportunity to earn time after each class period. It will be up to you whether you want to use the five minutes time immediately or save them for the last period [study time where in many schools students can work on their lessons or homework] where you can have up to 30 minutes of uninterrupted game time." The implementation can be tailored for the child or adult. This will avoid the expectation of being instantly gratified. If the student refuses to comply initially, warn them such behavior will result in confiscation of the phone for the day.

Today's society as a saboteur of behavioral interventions

Unfortunately when it comes to handling tantrums the main indicator of how successful a behavioral plan will be will depend on the consistency of implementation by all those working or living with the individual. Many factors must be considered when looking at how an individual responds inappropriately when not getting what they want. Family upbringing will greatly influence what and how corrective measures are designed to deal with the behaviors in question. In today's society parents face an enormous task of trying to juggle raising a family and providing financially for them. Many parents work two jobs in order to make ends meet and in many households both parents have full time jobs in addition to raising children. With ever more invasive technology creeping into our daily lives there seems to be little time left for quality family time. One needs to be able to give undivided attention to monitoring a child's behavioral patterns.

SOCIETAL DISTRACTIONS AS A SIGN OF THE TIMES

Here in the United States people can't even give undivided attention to driving because they are too focused on talking or texting on their cell phones. Many states are now enacting laws prohibiting cell phone use by drivers while driving due to the high volume of cell phone related accidents due to inattention. I wish more people would adopt my motto when I am driving: "If it's that important they will leave a voice mail message or call back later, but for now I can't concentrate on two things simultaneously so I choose to ignore the distraction of a phone call."

I marvel at all the people I see who cannot bear to leave their Blackberry turned off for more than a minute. When I fly I see more computers in use on the plane by passengers than books. Human interaction is taking a backseat to tweets, Facebook, and other means of technological communication. How on earth, with this technological mindset in society, can a parent spend uninterrupted time or even compete with the latest wireless communication trends when focusing on the behavioral needs and challenges of child rearing?

Handling inappropriate behaviors demands vigilance to observe and act quickly along with a commitment to enact corrective measures at the first sign of defiance. It requires all individuals in that child's or adult's life to be ready to enforce an agreed-upon behavioral plan. Please don't think that I am being judgmental or overly critical but during my seminars so many professionals come up to me complaining that their student or client is clearly misbehaving but all attempts to communicate that to the parents fail. Some parents hide behind the excuse, "Timmy can't help himself because of his autism."

Others say that with multiple jobs and other children in the household they just don't have the time to devote to correcting an inappropriate behavior. I have talked with parents who tell me again and again that it is just easier to let Timmy play with his smart phone as long as he wants when he comes home from school because that way he is quiet and not misbehaving. Timmy's teachers complain to me that they can't despite the best behavioral plan get him to stay on task or even be attentive in class because all he wants is his smart phone. There is no incentive for him to follow the plan because at home he is "rewarded" with his special interest in order to avoid creating unwanted drama in the family. I understand the parents' dilemma and honestly I have no answers on how to correct this problem brought on by a whirlwind evolution of technology, other than enforcing a strict behavioral program no matter how much effort it takes to correct the offending behaviors. I am not anti-technology, I am merely pointing out a need for balance. There is so much emphasis on an autistic individual's "obsession" with a special interest but when I look around I see most of society "obsessed" or more succinctly "addicted" to the newest technological fads to the point it interferes with daily life just as equally as an autistic preoccupation with a special interest.

If you have ever gone out to a restaurant to enjoy a break from this fast paced life with a quiet relaxing dinner I am sure you have encountered this "addiction" in more than one patron. A cell phone rings or (more correctly) plays a musical tune at the table next to you. Its owner, after fumbling to free this electronic marvel, starts off the conversation with something like, "Hey, how's it going? No, I am not busy and yeah, I can talk," and then proceeds with a lengthy conversation or gossip fest. What is annoying is that these people, because of the noise in the restaurant, can't hear the caller well so they talk so loudly everyone in the room can hear them. Most don't have the courtesy to at least leave the table and go outside. They can't even turn off the phone during the meal in fear of missing some important bit of news. I have seen families where they are all enjoying the meal, spending quality time, and either Mom or Dad gets a call. It isn't a life or death call and I watch as the parent then focuses an inordinate amount of time on the phone to the point there are either feelings of resentment or just resignation by the children that they aren't as important as the phone call. The younger the child the quicker I observe this restlessness of not being the object of attention turn into boredom which quickly manifests itself in inappropriate behaviors. By the time the parent tries to redirect the child's attention to eating, a tantrum ensues.

In fairness to parents I have also spoken to numerous parents who complain that the school system isn't following the behavioral plan for their child, sometimes for very similar reasons. Asperger's students in particular who are mainstreamed find themselves in overcrowded classrooms. With a teacher to student ratio of 1:35 or higher the teacher has her hands full just trying to keep the children on task and attentive. Often when there is a substitute teacher or a fill in one-on-one aide for a child, they may not be familiar with the behavioral plan, not knowing when to implement it. Some teachers and professionals are stubborn and set in their ways when it comes to acknowledging high functioning autism and Asperger's Syndrome. Their mentality is typical of the prejudice that I still face on a daily basis. They feel that if you look normal (i.e. no physical deformities), are mainstreamed, and don't act like the classic autistic child who spends their time just rocking and hand flapping and looking at the ceiling then you can't be autistic. Still others feel autism is a convenient label designed to excuse inappropriate behaviors they attribute to poor child rearing skills, so they may willfully not adhere to or implement an established behavioral plan put together by a team of professionals working with that student.

A ray of hope

I see a growing mentality of handing over child rearing responsiblities to the school system, but these are, hopefully, exceptions to the rule. Thankfully there are many parents in this world who are committed to making their children their number one priority and successfully integrate careers with child rearing. I am not attempting to portray a doom or gloom situation. Because I specialize in teaching professionals, caregivers, and parents how to differentiate meltdowns from tantrums and implement their respective interventions I frequently receive requests for behavioral consults. I hear all the reasons why the respective autistic child is having tantrums. I never judge or place blame on a parent or caregiver but merely focus on the most logical and plausible causes. By no means is society the major component in misbehaving children. I am just pointing out that the ever increasing demands it places on our parents will in time severely limit their parenting capabilities. It is becoming a contributing factor. Yet in the midst of all this I have only encountered parents at my seminars and lectures who are diligent and committed to rearing their child in such a way as to embrace their "uniqueness," yet not using the "uniqueness" of being autistic as an excuse to behave badly. They are not stagnant in their child rearing approach but are open and eager to embrace any new effective way that helps in extinguishing bad behavior while rewarding the good.

CHAPTER 7

Meltdown Triggers

Novel situations: the number one meltdown trigger

A novel situation means anything out of the ordinary. It is unpredictable situations or unplanned events. It is going off script or abruptly altering a pre-planned agenda. Novel situations will occur repeatedly to everyone throughout their life. They happen suddenly and without warning. Because they occur so unexpectedly the individual spirals into a meltdown so rapidly it appears to manifest instantaneously and explosively. A perfect example of an unexpected novel situation is when you are in the airport waiting patiently at your gate for the boarding time to commence. The board flashes an on-time departure and the weather is beautiful outside. Your thoughts keep drifting towards enjoying being home again after a long business trip. Suddenly the gate agent announces over the speaker phone that your flight has been cancelled; the plane you were supposed to fly in didn't arrive because it was grounded in its departure city due to bad weather there. This announcement caught you off guard, so now what do you do on such short notice about getting home on time?

AIRPORTS: MY PERSONAL NEMESIS

Most people, though upset, would still have the ability to brainstorm alternative solutions to such a dilemma. A person with autism such as me would be so completely surprised and taken off guard that our cognitive problem solving capabilities would be frozen into inaction due to the shock of going off script. It is the shock of realizing that your pre-scripted timeframe is no longer functional and there is no back up script to rely on. Having found myself in that very scenario multiple times I became fixated on how this development had ruined my timeframe for the day. I would immediately begin to cry over not making it home on time and then I would start to physically shake as the anxiety over not knowing what to do next would take over. (Remember autistic people try to revolve their daily life around blocks of scripted timeframes.) I became so distraught over the fact that I wouldn't arrive home according to my designated time. Now my timing for everything I had scripted out was completely ruined, not only for that day but the next as well. It wasn't an inconvenience but a crisis because I have limited capabilities with my own self calming strategies to navigate busy airports. These are a sensory nightmare especially when 175 fellow passengers are complaining, whining, and getting irate over the cancelled flight announcement. The "buzz" of their activity, which includes talking in higher pitches and volume on the cell phone en masse is excruciatingly painful.

I can only tolerate being in sensory overwhelming locations for a limited amount of time. After that all coping strategies will fail due to the fact that I need to "recharge" in a safe quiet familiar place like home where I can "feel" predictability, routine, and a sense of quiet. There comes a point where strategies will no longer be effective and the only way to prevent a meltdown is to remove myself from the location. While that may help with the sensory problem, it won't have any effect on my spiraling into an anxious state over not having an alternate plan to get home. Besides battling sensory issues in public I must also contend with the unpredictability of navigating the social networks once outside of the home. I don't think most people understand how difficult this is, especially when they see me in total control with no communication difficulties while I am presenting at a seminar or keynote presentation. They don't understand while I am speaking I am in a controlled environment that has been scripted to a point where I feel complete calmness and a sense of control. In an unfamiliar social setting I am a totally different person who is hypervigilant, rigid, and generally very reserved, speaking only when spoken to so as not to accidently go into a monologue about some special interest that ends up boring people. I calculate my every action and spoken thought so as not to come across as socially inappropriate, which is very mentally draining after a while.

I have learned self control regarding my autistic natural communication style which comes across or is perceived as blunt, confrontational, and non diplomatic at times, but in a novel situation I lack the mental concentration to remember how to communicate in a non abrasive way. As I attempt to extract answers from the ticket agent when we are both stressed I come across as almost aggressive in nature. That is not my intent but the increasing anxiety levels within my body gives rise to pressured speech and an inability to modulate volume. That in turn irritates the gate agent who decides that I am unable to communicate in a "mature" fashion and tells me she can't help me, so stand back and let another passenger come up to the desk.

In the past this has resulted in a full blown meltdown where I am crying, hand flapping, having echolalia, and exhibiting a myriad of physical manifestations of adrenaline overload. Subsequently I have decided to visibly display that I am autistic by wearing identification—I choose to wear a printed 4 x 4" sign encased in a passport holder around my neck, which reads, "I have autism." (Identifying oneself in this manner must be an individual choice based on that person's needs and limitations. It may not be suitable for every individual.) As a result I am spared the usual treatment of being interrogated as a terrorist by airport security and am taken to a less visible area where they are able to call an emergency contact person identified on my identification card. That contact person is usually able to work out an alternative route with an agent of the airline while I am with the authorities. Once my adrenaline rush is expended I am able to understand only that I have an alternate way home. Due to the strain of the meltdown I need to be escorted to the new departure gate. I am so worn out physically and mentally I cannot make any clear decisions immediately afterwards. After a meltdown it takes a good 30 to 60 minutes to regain most of my cognitive functioning abilities and during that time I need outside assistance to make sure that while in a "cognitive deficit" I don't harm myself through actions where I unintentionally put myself at risk such as leaving the airport and wandering aimlessly in traffic.

BACK UP SCRIPTS OR CONTINGENCY PLANS: THE MAIN STRATEGY FOR NOVEL SITUATIONS

The most effective strategy in dealing with novel situations is having a back up plan. Having an alternative script for the "what if?" syndrome when first developing the initial script for a particular situation will go a long way in preventing a meltdown. A "plan B" allows the autistic person to stay in control by having an action plan to fall back on should something go off script. In my case before I fly out to any destination I go online and look up alternate flights home. I write down the airline reservation phone numbers, flight numbers, and departure times and carry this information in my wallet when I travel. This way if my flight should be cancelled for any reason I know what alternative routes are available and I can book that flight by myself as opposed to waiting in a line of upset, impatient, and angry fellow passengers. While I will still react negatively to the news of a cancelled flight my thoughts immediately focus on implementing the back up plan or script rather than dwelling on the realization I went off script. This is important to remember because as I have emphasized, for us our life revolves around predictability and problem solving so as to stay in a predictable state. We react strongly when going off script because our plan for the day has been suddenly altered and we cannot adjust to abrupt changes. Knowing there is a back up plan to fall upon allows a sense of control over the uncontrollable. It makes the unpredictable predictable because it was a pre-thought out solution to implement so as to stay on track or on script.

"In the unlikely event of..."

As discussed in Chapter 1, one time while I was actually listening to the pre-flight safety briefing by the flight attendant (a non autistic monologue rivaling our autistic monologue in content, interest, and monotone inflection) it dawned on me she used the perfect phrase for my novel situation strategy. I have adopted the first part of: "In the unlikely event of an emergency water landing, your seat cushion doubles as a flotation device" as the ideal phrase for remembering to pre-script alternative or back up plans. When you utilize "In the unlikely event of..." while coming up with a script, you are building in solutions to the possibility of going off script. It takes into account the possibility of something happening unexpectedly (a novel situation) and creating a back up plan so as to stay on script.

A case in point

Let's once more use the example of taking little Timmy to the public swimming pool each week to swim. Remember that handwritten note saying that the pool is closed, which results in Timmy immediately spiraling into an anxious state, with all attempts to console him failing. Consider the following questions in light of this example.

Is Timmy spiraling into a meltdown solely because he couldn't engage in his favorite recreational activity of swimming?
No. Losing his favorite activity is a great disappointment that allows for frustration but isn't the primary trigger for a meltdown.

What is the primary trigger in this situation?
It is the novel situation of finding out upon arrival that the pool, which was supposed to be open, has unexpectedly closed for the day.

Why is this situation triggering a meltdown response?
It is due to the sudden closing of the pool completely ruining Timmy's script of how his afternoon was going to unfold. In his mind he had allotted a certain block of time for this activity and

scripted the remaining part of his day according to the amount of time he would spend at the pool. Now he has this void filled with unscripted time and no activity. No back up plan of what to do next, which is terrifying. Timmy feels completely out of control because he cannot anticipate what will happen next. This makes him feel vulnerable.

Seeing as this was an unforeseeable occurrence was there anything that could have been done proactively to prevent a meltdown?
Yes. Each time before setting out for the pool always create a back up plan just in case. Inform Timmy ahead of leaving by utilizing the phrase, "In the unlikely event of…"

In this case a back up plan would be to engage in another recreational activity that would still be enjoyable to Timmy. "Timmy, in the unlikely event the pool is closed for any reason today, we will go play miniature golf for the same timeframe and still be home by 5:00 pm."

While naturally feeling disappointed over not swimming Timmy is less likely to spiral into a meltdown because there is a back up script that will keep all his other scripts for the day on their respective timetables thereby not causing a sense of "having the rug pulled out from under his feet." I like that expression because if you visualize that actually happening to someone, you know they are caught unaware as they frantically attempt to maintain a fleeting balance and not fall as the ground moves under their feet.

MULTIPLE BACK UP OR CONTINGENCY PLANS ARE BENEFICIAL

It is even better to have more than one back up plan to ensure a feeling of security for the individual with autism. I found in talking to parents that their children, like me, will tend to get anxious even with a "plan B" when going off the original script, worrying about what if that plan gets ruined as well. It is O.K. to have many options available when encountering a "road block" (metaphorically and or literally) and really there is no set limit to how many are too many.

Incorporate back up plans within scripts so the autistic individual has some sense of an action plan to fall back on.

COMMUNICATING BACK UP PLANS TO THE SEVERELY AUTISTIC OR NON VERBAL POPULATION

This strategy is equally if not more important to utilize when working with severely autistic individuals and the non verbal population as they tend to be much more rigid in their set routines and react much more negatively to abrupt changes or novel situations. Don't be timid to communicate back up plans because they are unable to engage in conversation. Use the picture exchange communication board (PEC) system to give them a visual image of possible alternatives. For instance, non verbal Timmy has a "daily calendar" of activities he will engage in throughout the school day. It is a visual map of how his day will unfold. If Timmy goes to gym class for physical fitness activities every Monday at 9:00 am have a photo of a clock that shows nine o'clock. Next to the photo of the clock mark an arrow or use an equal sign to show the activity that occurs during that timeframe.

In many of the picture exchange boards I have seen, the symbols I have encountered most frequently are generic drawings of an activity or routine similar in composition to stick figures. While this is O.K., I advocate using actual photos of items in Timmy's life to give him a descriptive and personalized visual script where he can learn to identify places, activities, and items within his daily life. The most frequent cause of meltdowns in adolescent non verbal males revolving around masturbation stems from a not "concrete" descriptive photo to illustrate where such activity should be confined to if allowed. Usually for that sort of "recreation" I have seen either a generic drawing of a toilet or bed. Adolescent non verbal Timmy understands that to mean *any* toilet or bed. While visiting at a relative's house he may wander into the master bedroom and begin his "activity" only to be interrupted and reprimanded for it. He resists and then the behaviors begin. Same goes for the toilet. He may interpret that generic drawing to mean any toilet including public restrooms. Timmy truly doesn't understand why he isn't allowed to perform this function because he was following the visual cue on the PEC board. The simplest solution to avoid any "misunderstanding" of what is being communicated is to use actual photos Timmy can relate to. For the masturbation issue use a real photo of his bed or toilet in the house where this is acceptable. This will communicate to him very succinctly where he is allowed to engage in this activity.

Going back to the gym class example, most boards I have seen usually show only a generic picture of a soccer ball or basketball next to a hoop. Instead have an actual photo of the recreational activity taken at the same location Timmy will engage in this sport. To script in a novel situation such as a rainy day create a visual back up plan by having a photo of it raining followed by a photo of an indoor activity that would take place. Have another photo of a sunny day next to the activity that will take place outside. Use more than one activity if you prefer to let Timmy know there are multiple activities that could occur during that timeframe. Of course this strategy can be used in all areas of the PEC system. It is the most direct way of communicating that should a novel situation occur there is a back up script ready to prevent disruption in the continuity of his perceived timeframe.

BACK UP PLANS FOR THE VERBAL AND HIGH FUNCTIONING POPULATION

Let's go back to the earlier example of taking little Timmy to the grocery store. While scripting out how the excursion will unfold Timmy begins to ask a lot of "what if?" questions. Besides this being a plea for a more detailed script it is also his attempt to create contingency plans for any novel situation such as, "What if the store is out of milk?" "What if the road to the store is closed?" "What if you see a neighbor in the grocery store who wants to chat?" etc.

Script in ahead of time possible action plans to fall back on should any potential novel situation occur such as a road detour or the store being out of stock of some essential item so you must find another store. Script in back up plans into a routine as a safety measure by offering alternate choices or solutions to an interrupted routine or action plan. Depending on the situation, the stress level of the autistic individual, and their age, offering a choice between two alternatives may be beneficial in helping them to stay in control cognitively by focusing not so much on the problem but the alternative solutions. At other times even choosing between two alternates may be too much for the autistic individual to process so it will be up to you to take control and automatically pick the back up plan that you feel will best alleviate some of the stress level of the anxious individual. Always communicate all scripts and contingency plans before setting out so that the individual has an opportunity to either ask questions or mentally prepare themselves for going out into an uncomfortable social setting such as shopping with a parent or caregiver.

Sensory issues compounding the stress of a novel situation: a classic example

Novel situations can be intensely aggravated by sensory issues that are new or unique to the novel situation. A perfect example of this is my inability to handle the sensory madness that accompanies shopping at our one and only department-like store during peak times when it is usually very crowded, such as Saturdays, early evenings after people get out of work, or Fridays, which is payday for many. In my small town it is inevitable that you will meet someone you know who wants to stop and chat for a moment. During these peak times I have to contend with non autistic people who have been born with the disability of not being able to discern how much personal cologne or perfume is too much to splash on their bodies, thereby creating an overpowering almost suffocating stench to others within a 20-foot radius. There are people perched beside their shopping trolleys in the aisles preoccupied with chatting and not noticing they are blocking the path for other customers. Then there are a multitude of people who are going prematurely deaf as evident by their extremely loud and easily overheard lengthy conversations on the cell phone. Long lines at the check-out lanes where women who pay by check wait till the last item is rung up before rummaging through their purse looking for the check book. Need I go on about a multitude of sensory issues?

I have personal limits to how much sensory overload I can tolerate. My personal strategy is to shop during off hours such as Sunday morning when people are still in church, just before closing, or first thing in the morning. This works out well as I always have a list of targeted items I am after and don't feel the need to linger or browse what is new or on sale. I don't shop; I go on a procuring mission for specific needed articles.

A novel situation for me would be to have to go into the store during peak hours to purchase a necessary item that cannot wait till another time. Let's assume that I had to visit the Emergency Room at our local hospital on Saturday afternoon because I had an ear infection. They write out a prescription for antibiotics which I must take to the pharmacy to be filled. This happens to be in the middle of this one and only store. An unforeseen sensory complication that would already compound the stress of going in at peak hours would be the fact that I must get my prescription filled at this store on Saturday afternoon, which is Christmas Eve, two hours before the store closes for the Christmas holidays.

What would be some extra sensory issues I would have to endure above and beyond the peak shopping hours?
Definitely an extra measure of last minute shoppers making the store more crowded. More noise, getting accidently bumped, pre-Christmas sales on Christmas items, much longer lines at the check-out registers, and tension in the air from frazzled shoppers, just to name a few. I see very little Christmas spirit when only two pre-made, prefilled Christmas gift baskets are left standing on the shelf and three desperate last minute Christmas shoppers who decide they are entitled to one of the baskets lunge after them simultaneously.

From a distance it almost looks like a three-way wrestling match. This entire sensory overload piles on top of the normal sensory issues I would have to endure for such an establishment on any given peak shopping hour day.

STRATEGIES TO PREVENT A MELTDOWN IN THIS COMPLICATED NOVEL SITUATION

The first and most critical strategy would be to accept my limitations and not even attempt to go despite a myriad of coping tools to try to block out the sensory issues. Under normal circumstances they may work but in this complicated novel situation they have failed for me.

This is what I have done successfully to deal with this very crisis:

1. See if the hospital can dispense enough medication to get you by from their pharmacy until after the holidays when you can go in during non peak times.

2. Call the prescription into the pharmacy and ask how much exactly it would cost to pick it up and what time it would be ready.

3. If no one can go in to the store for me I would ask the pharmacy if they can drop the filled prescription off at the customer service desk which is located off to the right just inside the main entrance.

4. Before I go in to the store to pick up my medication I have either a check already filled out or the correct amount in cash to give to the register clerk.

Trying to push an individual's limit by forcing them to engage in a situation they know they can't handle can lead to a meltdown before ever entering the store just over the anticipation and worry of having to be in such an environment.

YOU CAN'T PREPARE FOR ALL NOVEL SITUATIONS

I have come across professionals and caregivers who have told me that they layered scripts with contingency plans for just about every potential novel situation so they feel they have eliminated any possibility of a novel situation causing a meltdown. If only it was that simple—but it isn't. You can't predict or plan for every novel situation because then it wouldn't be a novel situation. Despite the best plans and following routines and patterns very precisely something will occur that you never envisioned. Be prepared to be unprepared at some point in time. This is very important for the autistic person to understand so as to prevent feelings of personal failure when they aren't able to stop a meltdown despite the best self calming strategies.

When dealing with novel situations remember:

1.   You can't prepare for them all.

2.   Sensory triggers may complicate a novel situation.

3.   Back up plans or scripts are your number one strategies.

Transitions: another major contributor to meltdown

Transition means a change, whether it is from place to place or thought to thought. For autistic individuals of all ages a transition requires us to move out of a comfortable place where we feel secure, be it a physical place or a place in our minds. Being creatures that prefer a static environment, transition means fluidity which accompanies any shift or move and brings with it the element of unpredictability which we dread. There is a sense of insecurity and the unknown surrounding a transition, so many autistic individuals will automatically be reluctant to embrace such a move with the same enthusiasm as encountered by non autistic people. Also once overly focused on a topic or subject it is difficult to switch to another entirely different area whether it is in conversation, lesson, or special interest. It is our natural inclination to focus on one thing at a time giving it our full attention.

Transitions are another leading cause of meltdowns because they involve change of some sort.

TRANSITIONING FROM CLASS TO CLASS

Next to novel situations transitions rank second in terms of being a meltdown contributor. Any sort of transition requiring a change in environment can be very stressful. Let's take transitioning from one class to the next in a school setting. When the autistic student first arrives at class it takes a little time for them to settle in and adjust to a different environment. Many will create rituals ranging from barely noticeable to extreme during this settling in period. This is done as a coping strategy to feel predictable and familiar in the environment. Looking at the intensity or elaborateness of this ritual will tell you exactly how stressed they are upon arriving. Use this as a key in assessing their overall mental status. Arriving at school stressed can be an indicator that this individual may have only limited reserves when it comes to self regulating behaviors. Once they have adjusted to this environment it is almost time to go to the next class. It is a stressful time because with each move the student feels "uprooted" and must acclimatize themselves all over again, time after time. Complicate that by factoring in just how noisy and crowded the school hallways are during that time. With wall to wall students, banging clanking lockers, and students laughing and talking loudly, getting from one class to the next is a sensory nightmare. Usually when the bell sounds to mark the ending of a period, heralding a mass exodus from class to class, autistic students are faced with the challenge of not only controlling their instinctual response to overwhelming sensory issues, but also trying to stay focused on getting to the next class. Many autistic students and adults find it difficult if not impossible to carry on a conversation or even acknowledge when someone is speaking to them during this time because all their energy is focused on trying to not be overwhelmed and distracted by all the sensory triggers. At best they are perceived as non social and driven to get to the next class because of being so overly focused on blocking out extraneous stimuli. This stress can build up slowly over the course of the day, or even the week, until their mental energies are so depleted they lack the stamina to do it one more time and a meltdown ensues. Sometimes when an individual is dealing with a stressful situation elsewhere in their lives a simple transition like moving from class to class can be just the catalyst for a meltdown due to accumulated stress from other factors.

The easiest strategy to help the individual navigate a class change is to allow the student to leave a few minutes earlier, before the bell rings, so that they can calmly walk down the hallway to get to the next class. By doing this you eliminate 90 percent of the sensory overload triggers associated with overcrowding. It will decrease the anxiety associated with the anticipation of all the possible hallway interruptions that normally accompanies this transition. Being able to navigate the hallways before they become filled with students allows the individual to mentally prepare for the next class in peace.

TRANSITIONING TO A DIFFERENT SUBJECT

Believe it or not this occurs very frequently, yet its root cause goes undetected. Autistic Timmy arrives in your English class totally preoccupied with his previous math class assignments. He is not paying attention to you and all attempts to refocus him fail. Firmly you order him to put away his math problems or face losing a privilege or getting a detention. Timmy becomes visibly distraught over this and finally spirals into a full blown meltdown. In fact the intense anxiety began in Timmy's math class just prior to transitioning into your English class. The math teacher, Mr. Smith, finished his lesson ten minutes early, so rather than allowing the class to become unruly he gave them an impossible number of math problems to finish knowing that they couldn't possibly complete them before the bell rang. The point of this command was not to complete all of the math problems but just an exercise designed to keep the students busy until it was time to leave for the next period. Autistic

Timmy, however, feels compelled to finish all the problems because Mr. Smith's instructions were to complete 20 math problems. Most of the other students are aware that this is an exercise not meant to be completed so they can easily put away the math book and forget finishing the rest of the problems once it is time to go to the next class. It is an unwritten rule. Timmy took the math teacher literally, being unfamiliar with subtle non-directly communicated social rules. He is visibly stressed as he enters your classroom fretting over how just the move to your class is interfering with his concentration on solving the math questions. Being so overly focused on problem solving Timmy can't transition to an entirely different subject with unfinished business (the 20 math problems) on his mind.

Obviously the best intervention here is to make sure such assignments are better worded so as to communicate clearly to the autistic student the intent of the exercise. Rather than saying, "Class, your assignment now is to do the 20 math problems on page ten," try, "Class, your assignment now is to do as many math problems on page ten as you can until the bell rings. You don't have to complete all 20."

If you have a student who comes in unable to focus try to assess if there was any sort of unfinished assignments or topics from the previous class that may be creating anxiety. Be sure to be mindful of the fact that many autistic students once engaged in a task have great difficulty just leaving it unfinished and moving on to something different.

Sometimes a student may come in nervous; they are fretting about the upcoming lesson because it is too difficult for them to understand. In this case the student may attempt to stay focused on their special interest or be totally disinterested in learning and unable to be redirected. When pushed to pay attention they become highly agitated and may spiral into a meltdown. I remember during my school days how difficult it was for me to transition to math class from English class. I enjoyed English but being undiagnosed at the time with dyscalculia (difficulties with numbers) I dreaded going to algebra class because I was completely unable to grasp the subject. My math teacher wrongly assumed I was just lazy, stubborn, and defiant so he singled me out to write out algebra problems on the chalk board in front of the class time and time again knowing I did not know what I was doing. It resulted in public humiliation by my classmates. I would come to class completely disinterested in paying attention because I already knew I had no chance of learning. Half way through the year the school nurse diagnosed me with panic attacks that occurred during math period, but looking back I can say with 100 percent certainty that they were meltdowns resulting from unsuccessful transitioning from English to algebra class. I received a D- for algebra that year, and the following year despite my grade I was placed in geometry class.

The angst of anticipation in yet another non comprehendible math subject became so overwhelming that in order to avoid these "panic attacks" (meltdowns in hindsight) during math class I began a long career in high school of cutting first math class and then later other classes when I anticipated that the stress level would be too high. I was suspended from high school on more than one occasion for truancy and what was perceived a behavioral problem with frequent "emotional uncontrollable outbursts" (autistic meltdown) by my school counselor. Of course it didn't help my case when I constantly tried to reason with her that I was being misunderstood and not defiant. Perhaps my lack of social communication skills compounded by my bluntness of pointing out facts not relevant to the situation at hand (she was a woman in her late fifties who dressed like a young go-go dancer complete with the tall lace up white boots and I would bring it up during these reprimands that she dressed inappropriately for her position as a counselor) aided in her labeling me as defiant. I experienced countless transition related meltdowns during my school years but because I was undiagnosed with autism growing up, my only recollection of my entire schooling is one of heartache, misery, and suffering.

SUBSTITUTE TEACHERS AS A TRANSITION ISSUE

While I know so much has changed since I was in primary school, there are certain timeless challenges for every student during their school days. One of these is coming into class and seeing a substitute teacher preparing for class. This is sometimes an overlooked cause for potential meltdowns because it isn't seen as a transition but just a substitution. The substitute teacher is there all day so after the first five minutes of arriving in class the student should feel settled in to this environment. Unfortunately that isn't what generally occurs. When an autistic student is used to the same teacher every day they build a routine around the teaching style of this particular teacher. They begin to anticipate how the lesson will unfold based on observation of her since the start of the school year. After a while she becomes predictable and familiar. It is quite a shock for the autistic student to sit there expecting Mrs. Jones to walk in and then see a total stranger enter instead. This is a novel situation and a transition because it will require autistic Timmy to readjust to a completely foreign lesson plan abruptly and unexpectedly. Now the entire "routine" for this period is destroyed and the predictable patterns he had become accustomed to are gone. On top of that usually there is no clear explanation of why the regular teacher is not there. Answers that just convey vague facts like "Mrs. Jones is sick today" will elicit many more detailed questions about her illness from Timmy.

Ideally the best intervention here is to somehow be able to let the autistic student know in advance that there will be a substitute teacher for that day. If there was some way for the school to notify Timmy's parents the night before so they could prepare him for this transition or even if Timmy was told as soon as he got off the school bus, that would help ease the shock of going off script. They may still not like it but by doing this the likelihood of a meltdown is minimized.

OTHER TRANSITIONS THAT CAN CAUSE A MELTDOWN

I could write an entire book just about the different transitions that lead to meltdowns but I am going to only mention a few sometimes underestimated non school related transitions that could lead to meltdowns.

Moving from one home to another

At some point in life everyone ends up moving out of their home. Home is always a place of security and predictability in our hearts even in the presence of family dysfunction that may engulf this oasis. Moving is difficult for any child especially when it means saying goodbye to friends and neighbors with the knowledge that they will never see them again if the move is far away. For an autistic person this is by far the worst transition because usually it is abrupt (done on moving day) and permanent with no retreating to the safe haven they have relied on in their previous locale. Adding to the anxiety is the fact that at the new house there is initially no established safe haven or spot for the autistic person to regroup and feel safe in. It is as traumatic as being shipwrecked on an uncharted island full of poisonous insects and venomous snakes with no hope of rescue. Everything will be new: house, school, teachers, driving routes, stores, playgrounds, activities, doctors, dentists, occupational, physical, and speech therapists, just to name a few examples. To someone without autism, moving is viewed as just one experience incorporating all the elements of "change" that the move involves; for the autistic individual, moving is an endless series of continual abrupt changes with no end or relief in sight, which quickly becomes too overwhelming to handle. I can't stress enough that autistic people, including me, hate change of any sort.

The best strategy to help alleviate some of the stress of leaving the familiar for the unfamiliar is to do it slowly. Ideally take frequent day trips to the new area, stopping at locations autistic Timmy will be frequenting such as the park, school, stores, public pool, etc. This allows Timmy a visual of what will be part of his new daily routine after the move and something familiar that he can grab onto to gain a sense of predictability. The main thing to remember is to try to make the new surroundings and encounters as familiar as possible so as to create an element of predictability. Although it may not always be possible it would be very beneficial to be able to visit the new house just to familiarize your child or adult with the layout of the house, again for a visual picture of what to expect. Sometimes the sellers can be very understanding if you explain why it would be helpful even to just visit the backyard before the closing of the sale.

Be creative and take a pre-emptive approach by familiarizing the autistic child or adult with as much of their new surroundings as possible before moving day.

Transitions revolving around parental status

It is very difficult for any child to have to witness their parents embroiled in constant bitter arguments and even more difficult to grasp the concept of divorce. The non autistic child may be wondering why Daddy doesn't love Mommy anymore and may even personalize it by thinking somehow they are to blame for all the marital discord. The autistic child on the other hand wonders how this divorce will affect their daily routines. Their focus is not who doesn't love who anymore but on what activities and routines will disrupt them personally. It appears from an outside viewpoint as selfish and self centered and to a certain degree it may be, but it all comes back to routine and keeping life predictable. The initial fear is one of losing the familiar. Mom may gather the children on the couch to explain that the family will be experiencing a divorce. Most children will ask "why," whereas the autistic child may focus on "how." As Mother tries to explain that both parents will still have an active role in child rearing, autistic Timmy may blurt out questions regarding how the divorce will interrupt his daily schedule. "Who is going to drive me to the pool this Wednesday?" would be his first question after Mom explains that Daddy has moved out. Timmy's immediate concerns are based more on physical needs rather than the emotional component of losing a parental figure.

This is also true when it comes to dealing with the death of a parent. Autistic Timmy upon being told of the death of his father may instantly begin to worry about whether or not his birthday party will still be held tomorrow despite this "announcement." To an outsider this seems totally inappropriate, unemotional, selfish, and just plain wrong. Keep in mind our primary concern is keeping the "status quo" unchanged in our daily life. Any interruption, even a death, requires our problem solving brain to focus on reassuring ourselves that our physical daily routines will remain unchanged and predictable. It isn't that Timmy doesn't have the capability to grieve; it is just that emotional concerns are secondary to our primary need of maintaining predictability and usually the emotional component strikes much later, usually when least expected.

Going from one parent to two via a remarriage is another transition that is often very difficult to handle. If the step parent isn't familiar with autism or feels that the child, because they have no obvious physical handicap, are faking autism for attention, that creates conditions for hostility, resentment, and ignoring of the accommodations needed to allow the child to navigate through the day in a predictable and routine fashion. My mother remarried when I was only 12 and in all fairness to my late step father he didn't know I had autism. In hindsight when looking at all his behaviors and mannerisms, it was obvious he was the classic example of an Aspie (Asperger's Syndrome). We never got along, to the point my mother swore we were acting more like brother and sister rather than a parent and a child. His "routines" would frequently overlap with my "routines" and a battle always ensued over whose routine would have to be broken. We managed to find the triggers that always set us off into explosive meltdowns that my mother could not prevent or control. My step dad and I had very specific ways of doing things according to our own autistic needs and that was a major source of contention that lasted until shortly before his untimely death at age 46.

Guidelines for parental status transitions

Unfortunately there is no easy or singular answer to this parent dilemma. There are too many factors and variables to take into account. The only real piece of good advice I can give you is for you to remember that our number one priority is our own welfare. How will this transition impact our routine, activities, and other physical needs? It will be difficult for you to not feel upset by this lack of empathy towards your feelings but understand that autism is a cultural difference. We operate on a totally different wavelength. As problem solvers our primary concern is to find solutions so that our routines remain unchanged. Understand that dramatic change like adding or losing a parental figure will cause much distress due to being unfamiliar with this person's mannerisms and the unknown of what the future will hold.

Autistic children will often create very detailed rituals that require strict adherence as a coping mechanism to handle such overwhelming change. They may be more intensely preoccupied with their special interest with a tendency to be easily distracted or unable to focus. Sensory triggers may be amplified, and they seem to overreact to what normally wouldn't bother them so much. They may balk at the smallest of changes in diet or other insignificant matters of daily life. It is critical that you understand that children especially are unaware of how they are feeling and may exhibit behaviors that aren't "normal" but seem "off" for them. Try as much as possible to keep routines uninterrupted. Rather than making a sudden change, make small adjustments so that the autistic individual has a chance to process them one at a time, which isn't as overwhelming as all at once. Sometimes parents mean well by not telling their children about a dramatic change until the very last minute so as not to worry the child prematurely. We autistics don't like being blindsided and much prefer to see it coming. When it comes to explaining a death to an autistic individual, no matter what age they are, please be blunt and not politically correct. Avoid phrases like "Daddy's passed on," or "Mommy's in heaven looking down on you" because rather than consoling they are confusing at best and frightening at worst (more about this in the next chapter).

First time visits to the dentist or doctor

This is a transition that frequently ends in a meltdown and is one of the most preventable causes. While I am a believer in the use of social stories I do feel they tend to be overused without any other adjuncts in helping an individual gain an understanding of what to expect, particularly when it comes to medical or dental appointments. Simply creating a social story isn't going to give a clear visual of what to expect under these circumstances. It is like trying to explain what an ice cream tastes like to an individual who has never tasted it. The best and most effective way is to experience it yourself. The most effective strategy is simply allowing the autistic individual to become familiar with the dentist or doctor's office setting in advance of the visit so that at least the sensory part of the surroundings won't be so overwhelming. Use the process of graduation.

Well in advance of the intended appointment take the autistic individual to the office just so they can gain a visual and then leave. Next time increase that to meeting with the nurse or doctor, just to familiarize them with the people who may be touching them. Depending on the individual this may take only one pre-appointment visit or numerous ones. The rationale behind this is to give the autistic person a clear visual of what to personally expect as well as real time experience in getting a sense of the sensory issues accompanying such surroundings. You are allowing them to familiarize themselves, which minimizes unpredictability and not knowing what to expect in terms of procedures. Allow the autistic individual to ask questions and if possible let them handle some of the equipment like a blood pressure cuff or stethoscope. It is also important that a reward of some sort be offered for good behavior. Again, as I mentioned earlier, try not to use a tangible object for immediate gratification but offer if possible some privilege in its place. Avoid the temptation provided at many pediatricians offices of having the nurse give Timmy a generic type of lollipop after getting an injection. Having extremely "sensitive" taste buds many of us can detect the subtle flavor changes between the different brands of edible products. If the orange flavored lollipop doesn't taste exactly like Timmy is used to it could lead to a negative reaction. The best option would be to bring along the reward and then either give it to the nurse to give to Timmy or give it directly to Timmy yourself if you feel an immediate tangible reward is appropriate.

Other triggers for meltdowns

Anything that is sudden, dramatic, and overwhelming can cause a meltdown or catastrophic reaction. Ninety percent of cognitive meltdowns occur due to communication issues. Being in a prolonged stressful environment over a number of hours can also contribute to an autistic individual finally being unable to handle any more sensory or cognitive input. Sometimes while under this pressure it is something small that finally brings on a meltdown, like the proverbial straw that broke the camel's back. Autistic individuals may have an extensive array of self calming and coping strategies but those strategies have time limits for effectiveness. There is no other strategy that will work when the breaking point has been reached other than to remove oneself from such an overwhelming environment.

TRYING TO PARTICIPATE IN A GROUP CONVERSATION

I know a potential meltdown area for me tends to be completely overlooked by those around me. It is when I am in a group of people who are all having multiple mini conversations within a bigger conversation. Say for instance I was in a group of six women discussing my lecture on meltdown triggers. Two of the women branch out into a "sub-conversation" (my made up term for talking within a conversation on a related topic to a specific individual while the main conversation is still taking place among the group). They begin discussing specifics of how a certain trigger caused a meltdown in their child. It becomes very difficult for me to stay focused on the main conversation while trying to block out the secondary conversation of these two women. Next two other women in addition to the first two decide to engage in a sub-conversation. Now it becomes even more difficult to cognitively stay focused without becoming distracted by the extraneous vocalized thoughts of four out of the six in the group. If I am stuck in that situation for any length of time there will come a point when I can't process cognitively any more. Sensory triggers become exacerbated by cognitive overload from trying to pay attention and block out conversations and then begin to needle away at my reserve of staying in control. At some point I can no longer tolerate the situation and anxiety takes over as my body automatically begins reacting to being overstressed. If I don't remove myself from that situation I risk a meltdown from the smallest of triggers that under normal conditions could be endured without the same overreaction. I have talked with other autistic adults who have agreed with me and said that they tend to "lose it" after being in such prolonged environments more often than having a meltdown "out of the blue."

TIME LIMITS AS A SOURCE FOR CATASTROPHIC REACTIONS

Often when an individual with autism is given a time limit, as during a test, they become overwhelmed before they even start because they begin trying to ration the amount of time they allow per test question. If you are taking a test with 120 questions and you have one hour to complete it, the autistic brain automatically calculates that the time allowance for answering each question is 30 seconds. From the autistic standpoint, when an individual comes across a question they don't know, they immediately begin to focus on the time limit and how much time they are wasting on a particular question. Skipping that question and going on to another is a transition as it requires us to leave a problem unsolved and move on without closure regarding the unanswerable question. Our brain will automatically begin to obsess on how much time was wasted and how much is left and this will become the major focus of our attention. This is because the 30 seconds per question rule created a working script of how to budget an allotted timeframe and now that a question has left us bewildered, we have gone off script by using up more than 30 seconds on that particular question. Going off script for any reason is a source of great stress. This can be further compounded by time reminders ("Class, you have ten minutes remaining for this test") designed to help the student be aware of the time left for completion of the test. This only fuels our fear of having no working script to complete the test because of the lost minutes spent on the unanswerable questions.

When giving a test be mindful of this need to ration time for each question and avoid reminders of time remaining, which also distract the autistic student from problem solving, causing a break in the continuity of thought, which in turn forces us to start the train of thought all over again because we experience great difficulties in just "picking up from where we left off."

BEING RUSHED OR HURRIED TO DO ANYTHING

As I have mentioned throughout this book autistic individuals like me live according to timetables we determine and create through routines and rituals. In a situation where I am taking my normal time engaging in a routine activity such as washing the dishes and my husband is in a rush to go somewhere he will frequently begin to badger me with, "Are you almost done?" It is his way of phrasing that I am taking too long and to hurry up.

If I say "No" he will try to get me to cut corners hoping that this would get the job of doing dishes done more quickly. I have a certain "way" of doing the dishes which is yes, a routine with built in rituals of how the dishes get washed, rinsed, and dried. I like my dishes to drip dry in the dish strainer as opposed to wiping them dry with a dish towel. I have done it this way for the 23 years I have been married to him so this isn't a secret technique he is unaware of. I never leave to go someplace with dirty dishes in the sink. That is a rule my mother taught me as a child. His mother never taught him that rule so he feels comfortable asking me to just leave the dishes in the sink this one time until we come back. I can sense his increasing anxiety as he begins to hover over the sink area intently watching the not so exciting procedure of dish cleaning complete with the illogical strategy of staring intently at the dishes in hopes of doing that would magically cause them to clean themselves. Lord help him if he decides to interfere with my routine by grabbing a dish cloth to wipe the dishes dry as that elicits a strong negative response. Naturally, interfering with my routine, coupled by his constant reminders of how many minutes we are late, and his hovering over the sink causing me to be distracted from the task at hand, which slows down the process of dish washing in the first place, causes rising anxiety levels within my body so that I begin to instinctively react and feed into his anxiety. Before you know it I find myself so severely stressed that I am unable to focus on our excursion and then minor triggers of all sorts that I normally could block out become potential meltdown triggers.

Keep in mind rushing and hurrying forces us to go off script by altering the timeframe we created for the activity or thought pattern in question. The strategy is pretty obvious…try not to rush us. If time is an issue, try setting the timeframes so that you incorporate extra time for these exact activities in question. Build in extra minutes if possible. It is not beneath my husband's dignity to set the kitchen clock ahead 15 minutes without my knowing it in the morning of the excursion with the apparent rigid departure schedule he set for us.

To sum up the major potential triggers involved in meltdowns and catastrophic reactions I have created a list in a quick and easy to read format. Please be aware that there are literally hundreds of potential triggers unique to your individual that won't all be listed below. Just because you don't see a trigger that causes a meltdown in the person you are with on my list doesn't mean that isn't a valid trigger. I have only given you general guidelines of how triggers may be grouped.

Meltdown and catastrophic reaction triggers

1. Sudden abrupt changes (novel situations).

2. Transitions.

3. Sensory overload.

4. Cognitive overload.

5. Being given too many choices at once.

6. Vague or unclear instructions and/or commands.

7. Being asked open ended questions that are too broad.

8. Being forced to be in a prolonged stressful environment.

9. Being in a stressful setting or situation without any calming tools.

10. Being given an unrealistic task that exceeds capabilities or limitations.

11. Going to or being the center of a surprise party.

12. Crowded places and/or events and activities with a high noise level.

13. Being rushed or hurried to do or finish something.

14. Miscommunications:

    a) not understanding the meaning of a metaphor

    b) not using concrete, precise, and literal language

    c) not getting understandable answers to questions

    d) using literal timeframes in a way open to interpretation, such as "Wait a minute."

15. Being given a time limit (i.e. you have one hour to complete this biology test).

16. Going off script.

17. Being forced to socialize during lunch periods at school (for a lot of autistic individuals our goal at meal times is to concentrate on eating, and following or participating in conversations during that time is very distracting and annoying).

I would like to comment on trigger number 17. It is a common social skill teaching strategy to have the autistic student socialize during lunch or any meal time with their peers. This can be extremely difficult if not impossible for some students because it requires them to focus on multiple things like eating, listening, making some sort of eye contact, processing what was said, and thinking of a response.

Concentrating on listening to what someone is saying (auditory sense), eating (tactile sense), and trying to maintain some form of eye contact (visual sense) requires the use of three senses simultaneously, which can be impossible if you have sensory integration difficulties, which most autistic individuals have to some degree. I know this strategy is used with the best of intentions so I sincerely recommend that this be utilized on a case by case basis. There may be some students who wish to socialize and truly want to gain the appropriate social skills to do so, but I know of more students who absolutely dislike the idea of carrying on a conversation with someone else while concentrating on eating.

HORMONAL INFLUENCES AND MELTDOWNS

I have given you the most common triggers for meltdowns and catastrophic reactions. Obviously the triggers are as numerous as the grains of sand that make up a beach. Each individual will have their own unique triggers, so become familiar with the child or adult you are working with and spend time with. Just because they seem to be in a good frame of mind while working with you in a controlled environment, something as simple as taking them out for a walk could trigger a meltdown due to any one or a combination of triggers I mentioned. Sometimes an individual can handle one stressor but when it is combined with other stressors the burden can be too great and lead to an overload of either cognitive or sensory issues. Remember too that autistic children and adults can have a "bad day" where they respond negatively to an otherwise positive environment or task just because they are in a foul mood.

With teenagers you will find hormonal changes in both girls and boys which will alter their mood without any apparent traceable cause. Hormonal changes are different from teenager to teenager so be sure to take this issue in consideration when an autistic student comes to school in a contrary mood. Know the student you are working with. Mom and Dad, if Timmy wakes up in a defiant or cranky mood it may be just a case of hormonal flux. If Timmy has extreme negative reactions and even meltdowns over trivial or familiar situations and you cannot pinpoint the source of this distress it could be a hormonal thing. Just ask any parent of any teenager, autistic or not, and you will hear horror stories of their perfect angel who woke up one day at age 12 or 13 and had mentally morphed into "She-devil," or a "He-beast." Your child or student isn't becoming any more autistic; their bodies are responding just as normally as other children who aren't autistic. Setbacks in behavior should be put in perspective and not seen as a personal failure on the part of the adult living or working with this individual. It is also unfair to expect the autistic pubescent individual always to be able to ignore the strong impulses brought on by hormones and not allow it to affect them at all.

CHAPTER 8

Communication Triggers that Cause Meltdowns

Miscommunications are just as prevalent in the non verbal population

I decided to devote an entire chapter to communication as a source of meltdowns because in my personal and professional experience I have found that 90 percent of cognitive meltdowns are due to communication or, more correctly, miscommunication issues. Communication triggers are actually just as prevalent in the non verbal autistic population for two particular reasons. The first being that sometimes people who interact with the non verbal individual treat the child or adult as if they were still two years old and "talk down" (using words and tone inflection in the same way you would for a toddler) to them. Usually this tone is used innocently by people who don't work or live with the autistic person and wrongly assume non verbal means low I.Q.

The other main reason is exactly the same reason as for high functioning and Asperger's individuals: using vague non concrete language that isn't specific. Just because an individual cannot speak doesn't mean that their intelligence isn't just as developed as a verbal individual of their age. In this chapter the communication triggers I will point out as a source for a potential meltdown will apply equally to those caregivers and professionals working with the non verbal population and those working with the high functioning and Asperger's population.

In my personal experience novel situations are the number one source of catastrophic reactions, but becoming frustrated and anxious when I don't understand what a person is trying to communicate to me and being misunderstood leads to such anxiety that unless there is an intervention it generally escalates into a meltdown as I lose the mental strength to try to convey my concerns in a way that is comprehendible to the other person. The language barrier in these circumstances feels as though I am speaking in a totally foreign tongue despite the other person speaking the same language as myself. Miscommunication for me is the second cause for my cognitive meltdowns. Part of the difficulty lies in different communication styles between the autistic and non autistic mindsets.

Autistic communication differences

1. A LARGE FACTUAL KNOWLEDGE BASE

Before we can look at communication triggers for meltdowns we need to understand the difference in communication styles of the autistic population. For one thing autistic individuals have a large factual knowledge base and prefer to converse in facts. We love gathering facts and data. Part of the thrill of our special interest is learning all the facts and details possible about that particular subject. We enjoy (perhaps to the non autistic person a little too much) sharing these facts with others because we find them amazingly and even profoundly relevant to daily life. To us there is no such thing as too much knowledge in an area that holds a special interest for us. Unfortunately, often our "zeal" to share these facts with others is perceived as a rambling monologue. I have met so many Asperger's children who are just anxiously waiting for the moment where they can share these facts with me after going through the appropriately taught social skill greeting sequence revolving around saying hello, and asking how I am. Whether it is Thomas the train, or dinosaurs, I offer them an opportunity to share all the exciting tidbits they wish within my conversation time with them because I know that talking about special interests is calming because it helps reduce the anxiety of continually communicating in a style foreign to them. It also affirms them and adds to their sense of self worth because these children often don't fit in with their peers, and with the special education services they receive may be perceived wrongly by other classmates as being stupid or mentally challenged. By allowing these individuals time to share the wealth of knowledge they possess in their special area, it also helps them to reach beyond their comfort zone of preferring solitary pursuits to become more at ease interacting on a social level.

Dealing with fears by acquiring facts

Because we are more logically than emotionally based many of us will deal with our fears by acquiring knowledge in order to explain the reasons for our fear and then come up with scripts based on facts to deal with the fear.

Let's look at the fear of flying. Like many other adults I have a fear of flying. I began doing my own survey of non autistic people who have this same fear. The number one reason for this phobia is the same reason I fear flying: being in or dying in a plane crash. When I then ask them how they handle this fear I get a very emotionally based response. Some have told me that they absolutely refuse to fly at all because they don't want to risk dying in a plane disaster. Others said that they would medicate themselves before boarding a plane through prescribed drugs or drinking alcohol so as to "not care" or "take the edge off" whatever happens in flight. Most have sought some sort of professional counseling to talk about the emotional component of their air travel phobia which they have confessed aided only a little in alleviating their fears. A very common approach of the non autistic population is to seek comfort by confiding in others and hearing words of encouragement and reassurance from those around them that the odds of being in a plane crash are miniscule. This allows them to vocalize and talk through their negative "feelings" so as to gain emotional control over this sense of helplessness and powerlessness in a disaster. Unconsciously they are open and receptive to half truths which is a polite way of not revealing the all the facts that would correctly justify their fear. Such a classic response would be, "Don't worry dear, more people die in automobile crashes each year than in plane crashes."

While that may bring comfort to some non autistics, my autistic response to that comment would be more concrete: "Yes, while that is true, it only takes one plane crash with me in it to ruin my whole day."

Perhaps the non autistic person would benefit from reassuring comments that give them some semblance of security but to an autistic person such a comment comes across as almost argumentative and challenging. Words of comfort are useless to us and a waste of breath. We need hard facts and statistics to feel reassured. I love my mother dearly but when I talk to her on the phone about an upcoming flight she tries to lessen my fears by using her favorite reassuring phrase, "Dear, when it is your time to go, then it's time to go and nothing can stop that."

That does nothing to quench my flying phobia or make me feel more reassured so I manage to counter her statement by saying, "But Mom, if it is the pilot's time to go, then I am going down with him as collateral damage!"

Like so many fellow autistic individuals I deal with my fear by researching facts and statistics. In my case I acquired as much data as was available to the public about plane crashes and disasters. I looked into what caused the crash, who, how, and why passengers survived despite all the odds. I then viewed safety ratings for each airline along with track records of past in flight incidents as well as the model of each plane to determine which would have the least likely chance of encountering a malfunction that could potentially be deadly. Thank God for the internet, as it serves as a cornucopia of information on every topic imaginable to mankind. Naturally I found out many interesting statistics that I felt should be shared with anyone who would listen, in particular fellow passengers, but alas my conversational exchanges about this were never popular and seen as morbid. My enthusiasm and excitement in discussing this subject was interpreted as totally socially inappropriate. What they didn't recognize was the fact that my cheerfulness surrounding plane crashes was due to the feeling of self empowerment, for now armed with all this information I had created scripts which would increase my chances of survival, which in turn gave me a sense of control over the uncontrollable. Even though my chances of surviving are remote at least now I have an action plan for every conceivable type of in flight mishap which reassures me that I am going down fighting (no pun intended).

Trying to reassure an autistic person by using phrases that aren't steeped in facts is seen as insulting. Phrases such as, "Don't worry about it," or "Things will work out in the end," only come across as a minimization of our fear. That is not what we want to hear. To reassure us tell us a fact related to our fear that will help alleviate some concern over the great unknown. For instance to offer me a reassurance for the upcoming flight, saying something like, "You know your airline has the highest safety record in the industry today, and also hasn't had any major incidents while in flight in over a decade," will help ease my concern about getting on a plane.

That at least offers some concrete evidence (facts) which in turn would be perceived by an autistic individual as reassuring.

A teen obsessed with the macabre: a communication misinterpretation

People with autism will tend to seek out facts about a topic that causes them fear. Sometimes autistic teenagers will become "obsessed" with what is seen a macabre special interest as a way of "studying" the facts and developing strategies to deal with that fear through the use of logical countermeasures to combat the fearful scenario.

I was called in to do a consultation for a 13-year-old Asperger's teen who was obsessing over vampires so much that he began to frighten his teachers and classmates by going into gruesome detail on how to kill a vampire. His mother was horrified to find out that on his computer he had downloaded and created folders for so much vampiric blood and gore information. He seemed to delight in his recall of all the facts he gathered about vampires and their proper demise to anyone who was around him. There was concern that he might be exhibiting psychopathic tendencies with his rambling monologues of death and the undead. Superficially and based solely on his obsession, I can see how the school came to that conclusion and required that the boy undergo psychological testing. He terrified his peers by explicitly telling them in great detail that unless they protected themselves they could end up dead or worse. Whenever the teachers caught him trying to "convince" a fellow student that there were vampires in the school, they pulled him aside and ordered him to stop talking immediately. This led to him becoming paranoid over not being able to finish his conversation and developed into a full blown meltdown every time. Prior to his vampire obsession he had no history of such bizarre interests. After talking to the mother and finding out this "interest" just came on suddenly and "out of the blue" I already suspected the root cause of his behaviors.

While interviewing the boy he did come across as initially very smug in informing me about all his methods of destroying the undead. To some adults it almost appeared as if he was deliberately trying to elicit a shock reaction from them. Maybe because I am autistic my first impression was of him feeling confident, not bordering on insanity. I use my autism in this context because as the common expression goes, "It takes one to know one." I just "sensed" that he was compensating for a fear or phobia by using facts as a way to combat the overwhelming terror of not having a logical concrete script to deal with the situation. It is a familiar coping strategy in people with autism and I recognize when it is used in other likeminded individuals (autistic people).

I asked pointed concrete questions regarding the onset of his fascination with the undead. His answers revealed what I already knew but shocked his parents and teachers. There is a new teen cult following of a movie chronicle revolving around teenage vampires and forbidden love between a vampire and a human. In the United States this movie saga has had extreme effects on teenagers, going so far as developing cliques where they routinely engage in actual human biting and blood drinking as a sign of loyalty and friendship. This young Asperger's teen overheard a conversation during lunch about such an activity and witnessed first hand the bite marks on a fellow student sitting at his table. Curious, he asked the student what happened and the student responded in an intimidating tone by saying he bore the mark of a vampire. Naturally the Aspie teen became terrified over the thought that vampires did exist, so he desperately tried to warn his teachers and parents who unfortunately kept telling him that there were so such creatures. Convinced otherwise, he decided to gather as much information as he could on self protection from vampires via the internet and from watching vampire movies, intently studying the methods used to destroy Dracula. He then tried to recite the facts he discovered to the adult skeptics as a way to "prove" he had the facts to back his claim of existing vampires. Had the adults he confronted not initially dismissed his fear as childish and instead sat down with him and dissected his fears through the use of logical factual statements to the contrary, I doubt his obsession would of have gotten so out of hand.

In the end, once I uncovered the root cause of his occult interest, I recommended that he be allowed some therapeutic discussion time with a trained mental health professional, where an exchange of supposedly factual information regarding the existence of vampires that the teen collected be reviewed along with factual evidence proving that they did not exist. One problem was that the facts that supported such supernatural activity came from the internet. The teen in his quest to uncover information typed in his search engine, "evidence of modern day vampires." Naturally the only thing that popped up was the unlimited findings of claims supporting the existence of these nocturnal creatures. Under that search engine only information on the existence of vampires popped up and there was no information to the contrary. Because the amount of information on the topic was endless (more than 1000 web pages) the teen interpreted that as another "fact" proving that vampires must exist. The therapist during these sessions didn't "talk" about his feelings but actually spent time on the computer with the boy reviewing information found on the internet that disputed the existence of vampires. After a few sessions of this type of factual search the Aspie teen's obsession with vampires dwindled as he felt less threatened by the reality of their existence.

I want to point out that there are Aspie teens out there who have intense interests in the wide field of the macabre not as a result of trying to regulate a fear but because it brings them enjoyment for varied reasons. In the case study above, all the adults in the teen's life automatically assumed that he was mentally unstable, based on erroneous reports that there is a trend towards violence in some Asperger's young males, hence his sudden dramatic interest in a disturbing subject. Because so much of the issue revolved around trying to communicate his special interest to others it became a clue to me that it was more than a preoccupation with the occult. Before I label any behavior as disturbing I always make certain that I have ruled out anxiety as its root cause.

Factual exchanges are mentally stimulating

Besides using facts as a way to quench a fear, autistic people just enjoy a factual exchange more than the pleasantries of ascertaining the general welfare of someone else. Discussing superficial topics such as the upcoming fashion trends for summer or relishing tidbits of gossip about a neighbor or co-worker comes across as boring and uninteresting to the autistic individual. Being logically based our interests lie in what factual knowledge we can glean out of a topic rather than discussing the human condition. Our communication style focuses more on what knowledge or facts one can glean from a conversation that would either benefit us or add to our knowledge base.

If you don't believe me just try this simple experiment; find an Aspie individual and start a conversation about something impersonal but socially polite like the weather. A statement such as, "The weatherman forecasted rain for tomorrow but I can't tell if it will rain, seeing as it is such a lovely cloudless sunny afternoon right now." Chances are the Aspie person will reciprocate by stating facts on how to look for the signs of impending bad weather, or talk about some low pressure system that is heading in their direction complete with all the statistical data of speed, direction, etc. Generally speaking, even when engaging in "small talk," the autistic individual will have a natural inclination to interject facts and/or statistics to give "validity" to the conversation as a way to maintain interest in conversing and also to see if you can reciprocate with facts that they would find interesting. I really don't know of any politically correct or sensitive way of saying this so I will just be blunt; many autistic individuals don't care about someone else's feelings, so listening intently or compassionately to someone "vent" their emotions to them is as exciting as watching grass grow. Autistic individuals are uncomfortable in this type of exchange because they can't relate to the subject and will have a tendency to seem uninterested, interrupt and change the subject, or offer unemotional problem solving ideas when in actuality the other person just wanted someone to listen and not offer advice.

2. AUTISTIC INDIVIDUALS ARE MORE COMFORTABLE WITH "QUESTION AND ANSWER" COMMUNICATION

The second difference in communication style revolves around maintaining a conversation. Because everything to us is concrete, literal, and scripted, much non autistic communication, which is vague and open as a means to have the conversation flow, is too difficult for us to follow. For instance let's assume that you return to work after a three-day Christmas holiday. Co-workers may try to start a conversation with you by starting off with an open ended question such as, "So what did you do over the Christmas holiday?"

The average non autistic person fully understands that opening question to mean how did they celebrate the holiday and with whom? To the autistic individual, however, it can be very disconcerting and a source of anxiety because it is so open ended. They take it literally. Does that phrase imply that the individual wants to know everything they did over the holiday, starting from the moment they got up to when they went to bed each evening?

The question isn't specific enough and doesn't involve a specific block of time within the overall timeframe of holiday. Seeing as we prefer question and answer type communication, a better phrase to start the conversation would be, "So did you celebrate Christmas day at home with friends, family, or acquaintances?"

This way you have made the question very specific and not requiring a lot of mental attention to decipher its intent. Of course this may only lead to a one or two sentence response, because in the autistic person's mind they have answered your question, but at least it was phrased in a way that was understandable to them. Naturally if you want more details or the conversation to continue, it will require you to ask a battery of specific questions to gain information which would automatically be given by a non autistic individual with the initial invitation to them of, "So what did you do over the Christmas holiday?"

Sometimes the autistic person will answer your questions but not reciprocate by asking what you did over the holiday. It isn't that we are deliberately trying to be rude. We just don't reciprocate because it is a question we normally wouldn't ask and you didn't specify we should ask you about your holiday. It is O.K. to remind them that it is expected of them, with a phrase such as, "So, ask me what I did to celebrate Christmas day."

Communication as a main source of cognitive overload

Many common phrases in everyday communication can be a catalyst for a meltdown response because of their implied as opposed to literal meaning. Other words or expressions that are vague, unclear, and have no distinct concrete timetable are also a source of negative response for a large percentage of severely autistic and non verbal individuals.

The following is a list of the more common phrases or words that may cause an autistic individual to become agitated because of a miscommunication. By no means is it a complete listing but it will give you an idea of how to better phrase what it is you are trying to convey.

REQUESTS THAT IMPLY ABILITY AND NOT A COMMAND

"Could you please pour me a glass of water from that pitcher."

"Would you please pour me a glass of water from that pitcher."

To either statement the autistic individual may respond with "Yes," but then not follow through with your request. Why?

"Could" and "would" statements are not requests for an action but a determination of ability. "Could you" actually only communicates the question, "Do you have the physical capability to perform such an action?" It doesn't convey the meaning: pour me a glass of water.

"Would you" literally translated means, "Pour me a glass of water when I give you a set time to do so at a later point."

A key strategy to define the timetable as right then and there is to use a simple three-letter word:

> "Would you please pour me a glass of water from the pitcher *now*."

The word "now" automatically defines the timetable for this request as in the present. This way there is no room for confusion over the intended timeframe.

If you give a command in the form of a question, that too could be misinterpreted as simply a query determining only ability or a desire to perform that request, especially if the tone inflection has that implied: *"Could you please pour me a glass of water now?"*

So be sure when making a request, to phrase it as a command and not a question, and use the word "now" meaning to follow through on that request in the present timeframe. Make sure your tone inflection doesn't reflect as a question but a firm yet polite request for immediate action.

LITERAL PHRASES INVOLVING A TIMEFRAME MEANT TO BE INTERPRETED AS NON SPECIFIC

"Wait here, *I will be back in a minute.*"

"This will only *take a second.*"

If both phrases are interpreted literally the autistic individual may become very anxious when the literal 60 seconds expires and you haven't returned. Others may begin grilling you over how you can do something that only takes a second because theoretically that is an impossibility given our time dimension constraints. On the other hand, if these expressions are used frequently the autistic person then deduces that the statement has no validity because it has never been executed as stated, and decides to ignore the statement altogether.

This is a common complaint I receive from parents. Autistic Johnny asks his aunt, who is talking on the phone, if he can go outside to play and when. This interrupts her conversational flow with the person on the telephone so she tells Johnny that the phone conversation is almost over and asks him to "wait a minute" and goes back to talking. Johnny times her for 60 seconds and realizes she isn't even close to saying her goodbyes after 65 seconds so he goes out to play. The aunt hangs up three minutes later and notices Johnny isn't waiting patiently to re-ask his question. When she spots him playing outside she becomes visibly upset because he didn't ask permission to go out, which is a rule he is to follow. She calls him in to reprimand him for breaking the established rule. This is how the conversation typically unfolds into a miscommunication:

"Johnny you know you are not allowed to go outside to play unless you ask for permission first. You broke the rule."

Johnny responds, "I didn't break the rule. I did ask for permission."

"When?" asks the aunt.

"While you were on the phone."

"I told you to wait a minute and you disobeyed my instructions," the aunt replies.

"I didn't disobey your instructions at all. You said to wait a minute, and not only did I do that, but I even gave you an additional five seconds grace period but you just kept on talking and ignored me," Johnny retorts.

She reprimands him by saying, "Don't you speak disrespectfully to your aunt."

Then she scolds him not only for going outside but for being disrespectful in his attitude when he responded to her chastisement.

In all fairness to Johnny, he wasn't attempting to be disobedient at all. He did exactly what he was told to do in very literal terms. When questioned about his actions he made a valid argument against her claim that he used the one-minute phrase as an escape to break the rule by saying he waited a full 65 seconds and then went out to play, because in his mind he did ask for permission. It was implied but never explained to him that by asking he would have to wait for a response of yes or no. According to Johnny he followed the rule as it was taught to him and his attempts to explain that to his aunt were perceived as argumentative and defiant.

THE OVERUSE OF BINDING WORDS THAT AREN'T TAKEN SERIOUSLY

"I promise not to forget to call you tonight."

"I swear to God."

"You have my word."

"I wouldn't lie to you."

I have repeatedly heard people say that promises are meant to be broken. I actually kept a small notebook with me for a whole month and in my daily travels wrote down every time I heard someone use the word "promise" in a sentence to convey certainty. I did this in preparation for my book and I was astounded at how many times I recorded the phrase "I promise" used in casual conversations.

I bought a new truck this year and the salesman "promised" it was the best purchase of a vehicle I will ever make. How does he know it is the best I will ever own? Auto technology has advanced dramatically since I bought my first truck in 1989, which I still own today. Back then cassette stereo systems were the epitome of technological advancement but honestly it can't compare to the CD stereo system I have now. I find the crank handles to open the windows cumbersome as compared to my new push button window control. Who knows how much more autos will evolve in the next ten years, to be an improvement over what I drive now, so how can anyone promise my 2010 Toyota is the best truck I will own for the rest of my entire life?

Before I left on a speaking tour I asked my husband not to forget to cover the vegetable garden with a cloth on nights when the forecast was for killing frosts. He "promised" to remember and forgot, so I came home to find my garden ruined from the ravages of an extremely cold morning. So many times I have heard "I promise to remember" but generally people don't. Although it isn't done intentionally I believe in this society there is a tendency to say what you think another person wants to hear or use words that bind such as "promise" or "I swear" without understanding their full implication.

In the United States whenever a person has to testify in a court of law they have to "swear" on a bible that they are telling the truth. Even diehard guilty criminals will "swear" to tell the truth and then lie anyway. Back in 1996 a hunter trespassed on our property and was illegally hunting. When my husband and I confronted him while on a walk along the fence line to make repairs, he pointed his rifle at my chest threatening to shoot me. He went on to physically assault my husband by smashing a tree branch over his head and yelling death threats before hiding in the woods until found by authorities. When this went to trial it came down to the jury having to decide who was lying and who was telling the truth because my husband and I along with the defendant all swore to tell the truth and only the truth. Because he pled not guilty obviously someone was lying. He was caught in a lie on more than one occasion during his testimony about the incident. In the end this man was found guilty on all seven charges. I understand that swearing on the bible still retains its original importance for many people, but for others it is meaningless, and I find that difficult to accept.

Even a marriage vow is considered a socially binding solemn covenant between two people who consent with, "I promise to love and cherish...until death do us part," yet the divorce rate nowadays is hovering at around 51 percent.

The use of the word "I promise" to an individual with autism of any age is in their mind a binding covenant that you swore to not break. We take that word very literally and seriously.

I had this very discussion this morning with someone. At one point she tried to explain to me that everyone breaks promises from time to time because things change, and asked me to remember the last time I broke a promise. When I responded that I never have, she couldn't believe it and thought at first I was not being honest. I then told her that a promise is a vow, covenant, and binding agreement to follow through with something no matter what, unless there is a rescinding agreement reached between the individuals involved. I always weigh the consequences before agreeing to make a promise because it means I am bound by my word to follow through with what I consented to do, no matter if I have second thoughts afterwards. I don't make promises often and never in haste. When it all comes down to it, in the end the only thing we have in this world to ensure our integrity is our word. A hundred years ago a promise and optional handshake was considered a binding agreement. Today you can promise and offer a handshake but that is followed by a mountain of paperwork spelling out every condition and implications of a breach of contract. Why? Because over time our society has devalued the honesty involved in simply reciting a promise by premeditated intentions of breaching those promises. Instead of it being a badge of integrity it has whittled down to a trite expression.

I don't mean this to sound overly harsh or critical to parents, caregivers, and those who work or are around autistic individuals because I believe their intent is honest, but sometimes time gets away from them and they fall behind in their busy day and simply forget, or feel a commitment to engage in fulfilling that promise at some other time is just as valid as the original agreement. It is not.

A broken promise

Autistic Timmy is excited when at the dinner table he hears his father say that tomorrow he only has to be at the office for a meeting in the morning so he will be home early. Timmy takes this opportunity to ask his ever busy father, since he will be home early, if he would take him to the new exhibit of asteroid fragments at the planetarium. His father agrees, but Timmy whose special interest is comets wants to make sure this is a certainty and so asks him to promise that he will take him. Dad says, "Yes, I promise tomorrow when I get home we will go to the planetarium."

Timmy's all excited because his father "promised," which he takes as a binding covenant to commit to what he agreed to. The next day an excited Timmy waits impatiently for his father to come home from work early but as the hours drag on there is no sign of Dad. The later it gets the more visibly frustrated and anxious Timmy becomes. He begins to obsess on the worst case scenario of something happening to his father as the cause of him not coming home. Mom tries to reassure Timmy that those fears are unjustified but Timmy insists that his father promised to take him. (Often, especially with younger children, they won't be able to verbalize the importance of a binding agreement but will keep on saying something like, "But he promised" at every possible explanation of why the agreement was broken as an illustration of the seriousness of the agreement.) Finally the father comes home at his normal time to a very dejected at best, or angry at worst, son. The father then tries to explain by saying, "Something came up at work and I couldn't leave. I promise to make it up to you and take you on my day off."

For Timmy, his father broke a promise and as a result his "word" is no longer believable. Some autistic children in Timmy's shoes become very angry in these situations (deep down, this is actually hurt disguised), so they tend to display a myriad of angry behaviors. I have actually heard an autistic child scream at his parent, "I wish you weren't my father" in a very similar situation.

All children view their parents as God. To them a parent is someone to look up to that you can trust with your life. Children see their parents as infallible and all knowing. Children often generalize that mindset to adults who interact in their lives on a regular basis, such as relatives or professionals. It is childhood innocence that sees mankind as inherently honest with only good intentions. A broken promise by an adult is one hundred times more devastating than a broken promise from their peers. At an early age children learn the value of keeping a promise through childhood rhymes among themselves involving dire consequences if the promise is broken. When I was a young child in elementary school any promise made with another child was considered a vow, covenant, and non breachable agreement. We had to recite this phrase showing the seriousness of what we were agreeing to voluntarily: "I promise, or else stick a needle in my eye, cross my heart, and hope to die."

The crossing of any body part, like your fingers, while making a vow was considered a premeditated acknowledgement of no intention of honoring the promise in advance so as children we would stipulate that there were to be no hands behind one's back while making a promise. Promises are something the majority of younger children take very seriously until life eventually convinces them otherwise, but by high school there is unwritten understanding that promises will be broken on a regular basis. For some high functioning and Asperger's children and young teens, however, they will not be able to come to an acceptance that promises are meant to be broken. Many autistic adults like myself will continue throughout life perceiving a promise in its literal intent, as an unbreakable covenant. As an adult I now have the power to inform another person before they make a promise to me that I will hold them accountable should they breach that promise for any reason other than death or a rescinding of the promise we both agree to. This way I give them an option of not committing to something they can't follow through and I ask them to use a different phrase that still conveys their good intent but doesn't bind them to following through on that action such as, "I will try my best."

A child, however, doesn't have the option I do of questioning the following through capability ahead of the agreement, so I implore you as the adult to avoid making binding agreements unless you are fully committed to following through, no matter what. This means that if you promise to take Timmy to the park on Saturday and Saturday arrives and it is raining, it still means going to the park in the rain unless you and Timmy had a rescinding clause for the rain such as; "Timmy, I promise to take you to the park on Saturday afternoon as long as it isn't raining."

VAGUE TIME REFERENCES THAT MAY ELICIT AN EXTREME ANXIETY RESPONSE

"We'll see."

"Possibly."

"Maybe."

"If you are good," or "If you behave."

Autistic individuals, remember, need every minute of their day scripted. Using a vague non definable timeframe creates anxiety because they are unable to determine if your statement is a yes or no answer to their question, nor can they create a working timetable of events for themselves based on that statement. Timmy asks his teacher if he can feed the classroom's pet goldfish. The teacher responds with, "Not today, maybe tomorrow."

That is neither a yes or no answer and for a person with autism who lives in a concrete, literal, black and white world her response is perceived as avoiding his question altogether. To Timmy she left it with no commitment one way or the other. It is paramount to never forget that when autistic individuals ask a question they are expecting an answer that is concrete; either a factual explanation or a yes or no response. Open ended vague responses don't work well for us because they are perceived as not answering the question but avoiding or ignoring it all together. This will elicit a strong negative response in some individuals with autism, particularly those who adhere to a rigid structured regime, because it isn't concrete or black and white. To a person with autism the world is either black or white; never shades of gray. That outlook may seem overly rigid to you but it is how we think.

I have observed the frequent use of the phrase, "If you behave" with children of all sorts, autistic or not, in various settings. For example, an autistic student, Mary, is having difficulty settling in and staying on task. The special education teacher's aide tells her, "Mary if you behave then you can go out at recess."

Mary becomes even more agitated because there was no discernable timeframe for good behavior. If she "behaved" when? Right then and there? Later? For how long? What type of good behavior was expected?

A much better way of phrasing that same request so that it isn't a source of great confusion and angst would be to say, "Mary if you sit quietly and focus and concentrate on this task until you have completed it then you can go outside for recess immediately afterwards."

VAGUE UNDEFINED OPEN ENDED QUESTIONS

"How do you feel?"

"What do you want to do?"

"Did you eat anything at all?"

Questions of this nature are extremely difficult to decipher for an autistic individual because they aren't very specific. A very common phrase used when two individuals get together is "So what do you want to do?" It is generally understood in the non autistic population to convey the question of what activity should they participate in while together. To an autistic person it completely takes us by surprise. How does one interpret that question? What I want to do and what is expected of me when I am with you are two different things. What do I want to do about what? Do you mean what do I want to do today, tomorrow, the rest of my life, for fun, work, or as a joint activity? When and for how long? What do I want to do is not the same as what should we do, so are you referring to a solo interest or something together?

Do you see how the question only creates many more questions? It takes effort and lots of mental energy for an autistic person to translate and ponder what it is the other person is conveying. A simple question will often elicit a battery of corresponding questions from the autistic individual in an attempt to get clarity, which is often misperceived as just being pedantic. A simple question turns into a tedious exchange of extraneous information just to receive an answer to the original question. It becomes mentally draining on both parties after a while. When I run into this type of communication gap my tendency is to avoid any further contact with that individual or group because it seems to take more effort than it is worth.

When it comes to asking about the emotions experienced by an autistic individual, the phrase "How do you feel about that?" or "How does that make you feel?" seems unanswerable because we are detached from our feelings. Although we do experience the same emotions as everyone else, being more logically based it seems our brains don't recognize when we are feeling a certain way despite our behavior reflecting how we are feeling. Particularly if the individual is already stressed and you ask such a vague question it will push the frustration level even higher, causing them to verbally attack you for asking such a stupid question at a time when they are desperately searching for an answer. Be more direct if you want to ascertain their current emotional status. Observe their behavior and then ask pointed specific questions such as, "Are you angry right now?"

ADDING A YES OR NO, AS WELL AS ADDING A TIME REFERENCE, CLARIFIES YOUR QUESTION

Sometimes individuals on the spectrum will have difficulty deciding on how to answer your questions. Besides being specific there are a couple of things you can add to greatly clarify what it is you want to ask, so as to receive a concrete answer. This next strategy is ideal for the severely autistic as well as the high functioning individual. When asking a question always add a specific time reference for clarification.

Instead of asking Mary, "Do you want an ice cream cone?" add the timetable for this: "Mary, do you want an ice cream cone right now?"

In the first question there was no reference to when Mary wanted an ice cream. Did the question mean right now or later on? By adding the "right now" (or whatever timeframe is implied, such as "later this afternoon at 3:00 pm") you have narrowed down the question to a specific moment in time making it easier to answer.

To further clarify what it is you are expecting in response, add a yes or no after the question. This also works extremely well with individuals with limited speech capabilities. "Mary, do you want an ice cream right now, yes or no?" By doing this you have made the question concrete, specific, and answerable. There is no need on the part of the autistic individual to attempt to figure out what you meant by your question. It was very precise and black and white.

We rely on the spoken word because we are unable to pick up on subtle non verbal gestures, cues, or implied meanings. Since making eye contact and listening at the same time is an impossibility for quite a few autistic individuals, listening intently to someone's words is our only means of interpreting language with another. I liken it to the following analogy of trying to communicate with a blind person. I mean no disrespect to the visually impaired community but using this analogy seems to succinctly describe the difficulty autistic people have when language isn't concrete and concise.

Imagine you are taking a walk with a blind person near a meadow. You spot a couple of young calves frolicking near a tree with numerous butterflies dancing all about. It is such a pleasant sight you want to share this with your walking companion. How would you describe such a visual to someone who has never seen a cow, tree, butterfly, or even a meadow? You wouldn't just say, "Oh look at the calves being playful by the tree." That wouldn't be enough information for that person to comprehend a "visual" of what you are pointing out.

Instead it would require you to be very detailed and descriptive by giving as much information as possible to help that individual form a mental picture. You may start out with, "There are two young calves with newly protruding horn buds, waist high, mostly white with soccer ball sized round patches of black on both sides of their neck and head."

One has to remember to always be extremely specific and detailed when conversing with an autistic person. This will eliminate confusion over what it is you were trying to convey, and less confusion means less frustration which in turn keeps the anxiety level low resulting in fewer meltdowns or catastrophic responses.

WHY DOES THE WORD "NO" CAUSE A MELTDOWN?

This is one of the most frequently asked questions I receive from individuals working with the non verbal or severely autistic population. Just saying the word "no" to them immediately sends them spiraling into meltdown mode. It is difficult to ascertain 100 percent why, because obviously these individuals can't vocalize why that word is so upsetting but I believe it has to do with a lack of information. Having observed countless interactions where a caregiver, parent, or professional had to deny them something, I haven't noticed a negative reaction when they substituted the word "no" with something else. Instead of telling Timmy, "No, you can't have that candy bar," substitute the word "no" with something a little more detail orientated such as, "You can have the candy bar after we finish this task but not right now."

Sometimes "no" can be interpreted as "never" which is a word and concept that is difficult to grasp without any detailed explanation of why. The simple word "no" is too vague. Even non verbal individuals have an innate need to logically process requests and commands as best as they are able. Converse with them in the same detailed concrete way as you would with a verbal child.

A child may also bristle at the word "no" because of a sensory issue. Maybe somewhere in that child's life someone raised their voice or perhaps shouted "NO" at them, which besides being a possible sensory trigger (noise level) took them by surprise. It may not have been a family member or teacher but someone else who came in contact with that child. Unless you have that child in your presence 24 hours a day, seven days a week, there is no way of knowing what interactions they have with others they will come in contact with. A non verbal child cannot come home from school and complain to you that the bus driver screamed "NO" at him when he attempted to sit in the wrong seat.

I am not saying either possible explanation is always the cause of an individual reacting negatively to the word "no." It is just something to consider.

CHAPTER 9

Meltdown Interventions

In this chapter you will find guidelines for intervening in meltdowns. In my first book, *Managing Meltdowns: Using the S.C.A.R.E.D. Calming Technique with Children and Adults with Autism*, with the help of my co-author we took a pioneering training program I had developed solely for the use of interventions to avoid or reduce a meltdown in a medical setting and broadened it for use by anyone involved directly during an actual meltdown. It is a revolutionary book because it is written by a person who not only experiences meltdowns but has the educational background, training, and innate knowledge to understand how to effectively handle them and decrease their intensity when followed correctly. This book quickly became one of Jessica Kingsley Publishers' best sellers. I recommend that you have that book as an adjunct to this one because I like to refer to this current book as the "pre-quell" to my *Managing Meltdowns* manual. The book you are now reading helps the reader understand the role anxiety plays in our daily lives and how it impacts on meltdowns and/or catastrophic reactions. In this chapter I will expound on some general guidelines in meltdown interventions and discuss the appropriate actions necessary for effective management. We will also look at well intended but inappropriate interventions that could cause physical harm to the individual in distress. You will find more detailed intervention strategies on how to manage a meltdown in progress in *Managing Meltdowns*.

A word of caution: this chapter focuses on effective management for meltdown/ catastrophic reaction episodes only. It doesn't cover interventions for tantrums. For tantrums and bad behaviors please refer to Chapter 6.

Three main goals of intervention for meltdowns/catastrophic reactions

1. Safety of all involved is paramount

2. Reducing the stimulation level

3. Addressing the problem at hand

Warning: meltdown interventions will only work for meltdowns and catastrophic reactions. They will not be effective for tantrums.

1. SAFETY OF ALL INVOLVED IS PARAMOUNT

It is of paramount importance that safety be the number one priority when handling a meltdown or catastrophic reaction. When an autistic individual begins to spiral downward, so that cognitive processing is hampered even moderately, they are in danger of hurting themselves. Once the fight or flight response has been elicited they are no longer cognitively processing the world around them, they are totally unaware of their surroundings making them vulnerable to the inherent dangers around them. For example, if an autistic child has a tendency to run away from overwhelming stressors when in a meltdown they need to be monitored closely while in a playground next to a busy street. Sometimes just turning away for one moment can have dire consequences. Be aware of potential hidden environmental triggers, such as the sound of a siren from a police car or noise from nearby building or road construction.

With a catastrophic reaction, which occurs suddenly and seemingly out of the blue to the bystander, there may be no noticeable visible signs of escalating anxiety prior to the child bolting away from the playground. The child at that moment has no cognitive awareness and is reacting in a panic mode by fleeing the situation. They won't remember to stop and look before crossing a street; they will just blindly run into oncoming traffic with potentially lethal consequences. If you begin to notice the child becoming even slightly agitated, immediately try to resolve why, and if that doesn't reduce the child's anxiety find a secure place for containment, such as inside your vehicle where the child will be confined within a safe area as opposed to out in the open. Lock the doors so the child if escalating doesn't open the door to run away. Bear in mind that any autistic individual in a meltdown mode will lack the cognitive functioning to recognize how to unlock a car door. They may fumble or claw at the locking mechanism but to open the door takes a sequence of actions that requires cognitive thinking. Sometimes random hitting will unlock the door but if you witness them methodically going through the steps required for opening the lock then it isn't a meltdown you are dealing with but a tantrum. Meltdown interventions will be ineffective if it is a tantrum (if the child possesses the cognitive ability to problem solve to unlock the car door) so the only way to deal with the crisis is through behavioral management and implementation of consequences for actions.

The key for individuals who are bolters during a meltdown phase is containment in order to keep them safe. That means if you are in a room and the autistic individual wants to flee, your priority will not be to stop them but to close all access ways (doors and windows) out of the room. If you are in an open public setting don't wait until the individual is highly agitated before taking corrective action because time will be of the essence. You may not be able to predict at exactly what moment that individual will flee. As soon as you notice rising anxiety levels either focus on problem solving or begin pre-emptive safety protocols by removing the person from that environment to a place where containment is possible.

Safety also requires that you keep yourself safe. Don't position yourself close to an individual who is lashing out physically and throwing objects. Don't act as a barricade by positioning yourself in the path of a fleeing individual, because they will plow right through you and knock you to the ground. If you have a runaway don't attempt to give chase alone. Call out for help from nearby bystanders. What happens if you are middle aged like me and can't outrun an agile teenager by yourself? Individuals under the influence of the fight or flight response have incredible stamina and strength that you would not see them possess in calmer situations. How safe is the situation if you end up too exhausted to continue the chase and the autistic individual keeps on running? They will not stop until they either find a dark secluded shelter or physically burn off the excess adrenaline, which could take a while depending on the physical makeup of the individual.

I cannot stress this enough: an autistic person who is in the fight or flight mode will be reacting solely on instinct. They are unable to recognize familiar places, people, or things. Their actions will be similar to those of a terrified wild animal fleeing from hunting dogs. The autistic person will view anyone including close family members as a source of danger (like a hunting dog giving chase) and run away even faster. They are not in control of their actions or mind. The body is reacting out of instinct only. This is a very dangerous time when they or you can be injured.

Self injurious behaviors and safety

This is an area that frequently leads into further escalation while intervening. I am not proud to admit that when severely stressed I have a tendency to be a head banger. Any individual who engages in self injurious behavior such as banging or biting will not even feel the pain they are inflicting upon themselves at that moment. This is because when the fight or flight response is triggered the pain receptors of the body seem to temporarily deactivate. It is an instinctual self preservation mode carried over from our caveman days, allowing time to escape a life or death situation.

An individual who is inflicting self harm during a meltdown will not even be aware they are doing it. It is almost impossible to pinpoint why individuals engage in it because of the diverse experiences each one of us encounters throughout life that influence our behavior, in addition to these innate urges to engage in inflicting self harm. Setting out to discover the origin of a self injurious behavior has to be personalized to that individual and never done during a meltdown escalation. During a meltdown phase trying to appease someone by offering them favorite objects or distractions will fail. Why? It is because there is at that moment in time no cognitive thinking going on inside their brains. The most common intervention is the least safe one, which is to restrain the individual from a continuation of self injurious behavior. I have spoken to countless people, from parents to professionals, who have told me that every time they tried to restrain an individual in that circumstance it only leads to an increase in the intensity of the behavior with accompanying aggression towards the person trying to stop them. I have witnessed many such episodes myself where physical restraint had only adverse effects and didn't decrease the injurious behaviors. For the individual having a meltdown, their self preservation instinct is to attack anyone who enters their personal space, because they perceive that individual as a physical threat to their personal survival. Even Mom or Dad isn't recognized as anything other than a threat and they become aggressive to them also.

NEVER attempt to restrain an autistic individual from further infliction of self harm! They will only fight against your attempts and increase the intensity of self aggression and aggression towards you.

How do you control such behavior in a safe manner without restraint?

Of course I am not advocating that you simply watch from a safe distance and allow them to continue to hurt themselves. At the same time you must also prevent injury to yourself. Because they are not functioning cognitively at the height of the meltdown they will be unaware of anything that is occurring out of their visual field.

They will pick up on sudden movements and become defensive, so it is imperative that any actions you take be executed calmly and cautiously. Script your movements as if you were trying to approach a cornered frightened feral puppy. The object is to prevent further harm without touching them. Grab any soft readily available item to muffle the impact of the behavior such as a pillow, sweater, handbag, cushion, etc. Carefully, with soft object in hand, approach the individual from behind, being absolutely quiet. If the individual is a head banger then place the pillow or soft object between their head and the wall or whatever they are banging against. If they are biting or attacking themselves, gently place the soft object on the part of their body they are attacking. Keep yourself at arm's length from them, stay out of their visual field, and say nothing. If they are truly in a meltdown phase they will lack the cognitive ability to register that something was placed in front of them as a buffer. Continue with this until they calm down. There is no other safe way to deal with self injurious behavior once in a full meltdown mode.

Keep in mind that any form of restraint during a true meltdown/catastrophic reaction phase will only cause the autistic individual to fight against it more intensely. This applies to the verbal as well as the non verbal individual, whether severely autistic or high functioning. They perceive any form of physical contact or being in their personal space as a threat to their lives and will aggressively defend against any such intrusion. Remember they are acting on instinct and cannot be held accountable for their actions while in this state. They will match any level of aggression displayed towards them by raising their aggression level even higher. Do not restrain an individual for any reason during a meltdown other than for an immediate imminent threat to life.

2. REDUCING THE STIMULATION LEVEL

The second important focus on managing a meltdown after ensuring a safe environment for all involved is to try to reduce any stimulation that could act as a secondary trigger. If the individual is having a meltdown in the classroom shut off the overhead fluorescent lights if possible. Reduce the noise level by having all individuals leave the room. While I understand this is impractical and inconvenient, it is imperative that the autistic student not be affected by extraneous sensory issues from having other people in close proximity. I also worry that some individuals in that instinctual self preservation mode may perceive onlookers as a potential threat to their safety, and any sudden movements made in the general direction towards the spiraling individual will be interpreted as an act of aggression making that already stressed out individual combative towards the intervener closest to them. Ideally the individual when first beginning to spiral while still possessing cognitive functioning abilities should have been removed to a less stimulating environment such as a special cordoned off area of the classroom or a special separate room for them to decompress.

How you should communicate to a person in a meltdown

As hard as it may be, always speak in a calm manner. No matter what they shout or how violent their behavioral display, don't raise your voice for any reason. Raising your voice will only act as an auditory trigger compounding an already excitable situation. Use very short reassuring phrases repeatedly such as, "Its O.K. Deb," or "I am here, Deb." Make sure you say their name as this will help as a grounding aid for them. This is hard to explain to someone who hasn't ever had an autistic meltdown, but repetitive use of our name is something we can sometimes hear and recognize particularly when in the initial phase of a meltdown. Although we may not be able to react to our name being said, it helps us feel like we aren't spiraling into a black abyss alone. On a small level it offers a bit of reassurance that there will be someone with us this during the period when we are no longer cognizant of the world around us. Repeating the same reassuring phrase over and over again also acts as a form of echolalia. Echolalia is repetitive and repetition is calming as it is unchanging.

While an individual is spiraling into a meltdown it isn't the time to ask questions or offer choices. They are already cognitively challenged at that point and any interaction requiring more cognitive processing will only heighten their frustration level and expedite an impending meltdown. You need to be firm and take charge, making decisions for them which will ease the burden of them trying to function at reduced cognitive levels.

Don't ask the following questions:

- What have you been taught to do in this situation?

- How can I help you?

- Do you want to go out and play?

- Do you want to do something different?

- Do you need a break?

- Do you want me to call someone?

- Will you be O.K. if I leave you alone for a moment just to get help?

- Are you having a meltdown? Believe it or not it is one of the most frequent and ill timed questions autistic individuals hear while spiraling into a meltdown mode!

Any questions posed to them while in an escalation mode will only serve to further tax an already overwhelmed cognitive processing ability.

3. ADDRESSING THE PROBLEM AT HAND

The third goal of meltdown intervention is to try to correct the underlying cause of the meltdown. If the autistic individual is having a sensory overload meltdown from being in a store, get him out safely as soon as possible. Don't go back in the store once they have calmed down until you are able to pinpoint the triggers and have coping mechanisms in place such as stim tools or a key phrase to communicate to you that they are reaching their sensory tolerance levels. It may mean not going in at all. Find out if it was the volume of people in the store that triggered a meltdown and adjust your schedule so as to take that individual to the store at times when the human traffic will be much less.

If the anxiety levels are reaching the critical meltdown state over an unexpected problem, try to come up with alternative solutions. For instance, if I am waiting at my gate to board a plane and the flight gets cancelled, my anxiety level will skyrocket instantly to the point where all I can comprehend are simple short phrases. The most effective intervention would be to say that you will find me an alternate flight. Use uncomplicated sentences like, "Deb, I will help you find another flight right now."

Offering reassurance that you are committed to finding an answer such as, "Deb, I won't leave you alone until we until we have a working solution," will help in calming me down because now you have offered to make the unpredictable predictable. Remember when I am spiraling in this situation it is over going off script abruptly and all the unpredictability that comes with being stranded suddenly at an airport. By taking charge you are offering the individual in distress a solution, a plan B to circumvent having gone off script.

Autistic individuals will go into a meltdown mode if they go off script abruptly. Sudden and/or dramatic changes will be the catalyst. When addressing the problem it is best to have workable contingency plans and interventions before offering them to the distressed individual. There is nothing that will escalate the situation quicker than offering a solution before seeing if it is a real possibility. To have to go back on what you suggested as a solution will only send them into a panic mode and deeper into a meltdown phase, because in essence, in their mind, you can't be trusted to be of any help in this situation and all hope is lost.

When there are no alternative solutions

There will be many times throughout life where coming up with an alternate option to address the problem won't be feasible. In those situations the autistic individual will just have to endure the excruciating agony of not being able to rely on an alternate back up plan.

For example, you are driving your autistic son to school. Keeping routine in mind you follow the routine which allows autistic Timmy to feel that the drive to school will be predictable, therefore non stressful. Suddenly around the bend on the main highway, already congested with commuter traffic, there is a major car accident. There is a line of vehicles stopped in front of you to allow the emergency personnel room to work. The accident has blocked the road completely so everyone has to wait until firemen clear the wreckage. Behind you is a long line of vehicles so backing up the car to the last exit is not an option. It is a divided expressway with a concrete barricade, so turning around to head in the opposite direction is also not an option. Timmy, upon seeing the stopped vehicles, begins to panic over being late for school and missing his first class.

In this situation problem solving isn't an option because you are stuck where you are until the road ahead allows cars to pass once again. There is nothing you can do to change or correct the situation. Timmy is spiraling himself into a meltdown fretting over being late and going off his timetable. You must address the problem of him going off schedule before he works himself into a meltdown mode.

Timmy must come to learn that life cannot be predicted to suit his daily needs. The unexpected will happen and although it is very stressful he must learn to adapt to it by the implementation of self calming/coping techniques and tools. Having an autistic emergency tool kit on hand empowers Timmy to take control of the uncontrollable himself by allowing him to utilize whichever coping strategy best fits his needs at the moment. It won't be something he embraces for a "feel good" moment, but something he desperately clings to in order to keep his anxiety level from escalating. These "tool kits" must be personalized to suit the needs of the individual. It will take practice to become comfortable with relying on them as a self help strategy.

Autistic emergency tool kits for reducing the anxiety associated with impending meltdowns

An autistic emergency tool kit consists of stim tools as well as sensory objects and special interest items that have a calming or quieting effect on the autistic individual in an agitated state. Having been personalized to fit the needs of the individual, this kit is kept in a vehicle or with those entrusted with their care as well as on the autistic individual themselves. It can be as large as practical or as compact as one item. The main goal of these items is to offer a calming effect when under intense stress. It doesn't have to necessarily always be a tangible object. It can be a word game or time allowed to talk about their special interest. They are objects or techniques reserved only for anxious states that are proven to work in bringing a sense of calm back to the individual. During periods of escalating anxiety trying a new technique or stim tool to see if it will help can have disastrous consequences if it is rejected by the individual and only further serve to increase their anxiety level. We need something familiar because familiar is predictable and predictable helps us feel calm. Whatever is used should only be reserved for such emergencies, to avoid a desensitization effect if used regularly while not stressed. Generally speaking, regardless of the severity of autism, the autistic individual will already have chosen certain items that they cling to as a security blanket when stressed. Those are the items they gravitate to when anxious and those are the items you *must* allow them access to when in a state of agitation to aid in self regulation of rising anxiety levels. Those are the items to pack in such an emergency tool kit. An autistic emergency tool kit could include:

- Favorite music known to have a quieting effect on the individual, be it an iPod, portable CD player, or CD that can be inserted into a stereo system. It must be music tailored to the individual that they prefer when stressed (no matter what *your* opinions are). Relaxation music of waterfalls and birds chirping that advertise a calming effect will be useless to a teenager who would prefer hard rock to calm down with. Remember it is not about music taste or your preference, but about having a quieting effect on the stressed out autistic individual. Use what works for them and not necessarily what works for you.

- A soft fleece or any favorite texture plush stuffed animal.

- Any stim tool known to capture the attention and interest of the individual during calmer times.

- A small amount of a special fragrance they enjoy smelling. I look forward to laundry day because the detergent I use has a scent that I find irresistible and relaxing. There are times when I carry a small vial of this laundry detergent on me for potentially stressful moments while away from home. When stressed I inconspicuously unscrew the cap and take a whiff when no one is watching or excuse myself from those around me and retreat to a private place for a moment. It has a definite calming effect on me.

- Special interest objects that can serve to refocus and shift the thought process away from fretting over the problem and onto their favorite interest. If Timmy enjoys collecting shiny fire trucks then having one of his favorite (duplicate) fire trucks handy to give to him when stressed may redirect his attention from obsessing over the issue at hand. I used the word duplicate because collectible objects are often seen as sacred by the autistic individual and not meant to be touched, never mind handled, by someone else under any circumstances. Taking an item out of their "collection" will only cause an immediate extreme negative response or meltdown. It is best to either buy a duplicate item to leave in the tool kit so Timmy feels safe in the knowledge that his "collection" at home is intact. Sometimes you might be able to discuss in advance with Timmy the idea of packing one of his original fire trucks as an emergency measure when going somewhere or being placed in an uncomfortable situation. If he agrees then do it, otherwise don't disturb their personal special interest belongings.

- A favorite word game or song to sing together. While trapped in a traffic jam or having to wait someplace, playing mental mind games can help redirect their attention onto problem solving, trying to "win" a game as opposed to worrying about being off script. Be creative with these games. One word game I used to play with a friend when we traveled together and I became stressed over the volume of large city traffic was called the alphabet game. He would start by saying an object that began with the letter "A" such as apple. Then I would have to come up with an object that began with the letter "B" such as banana and recite "apple, banana." He would then come up with something that started with the letter "C" and recite, "apple, banana, cat." We would alternate letters all the way to "Z" and the object of winning the game was to remember as many correctly in order as possible. Whatever the game you decide on for a mental game, the point is to have the individual "forget" for a moment about the problem and engage in a fun mental game challenge. This can only be done when the autistic person is just starting to get anxious because once the anxiety increases to a moderate level they won't be able to function at full cognitive capability. At that point do not attempt any distraction requiring mental concentration or cognitive thinking.

Early recognition of signs of anxiety is the best strategy for preventing meltdowns

Don't wait to act when you see an autistic individual begin to exhibit visible signs of anxiety because that is your first and most important indicator that they are anxious over something. Unless the anxiety is dealt with it will only tend to escalate until it reaches the critical point of no return and a meltdown takes over. Because adrenaline is building up within the body, pushing the anxiety level even higher, you must attempt to reduce the adrenaline level by having the individual do something that expends that built up energy. The intensity of stimming will not only help in reducing the adrenaline level but also be a key indicator as to their level of anxiety. The more intense the stimming, the more highly agitated the individual is.

Physical movement as a calming tool for the verbal and non verbal individual

It is extremely important that you try to engage the individual in some sort of physical release no matter where they are. Physical exercise also releases endorphins which can help in calming down a highly excitable individual. Asking an Asperger's student who is in the early stage of rising anxiety to go and retrieve a box of pens from the supply room not only helps to burn off some rising adrenaline levels but also acts as a distraction from the issue causing anxiety because a change in environment, even briefly, may be just the reprieve the brain needs to stop spiraling downward into an anxious state. Use your judgment in determining if this is a plausible strategy by observing the stressed out individual. If you give them this task and they are struggling or seem to obsess even deeper about the issue causing their anxiety, then don't have them follow through with it. Their anxiety level is already too high for this to be of any use. Allow whatever form of stimming they need and if it is distracting to those around them lead them to a private place where they can have the time needed to stim in order to calm down.

As I have mentioned before, when I need to physically flap my hands when in a public setting to calm down I head for the nearest toilet stall, latch the door behind me and hand flap as intensely as required in order to self regulate my anxiety. If I drove somewhere then I would retreat to the privacy of my own vehicle. Utilize whatever quiet private area you can find during this situation. For the severely autistic and non verbal individual allow them to physically stim as needed and if possible offer them a small exercise trampoline to jump up and down on or exercise ball to sit and bounce on. Be creative and know in advance what sorts of physical occupational therapy tools will work for that individual. If you are traveling in a vehicle try some sort of hand motion such as clapping or flapping, and wiggling of the feet, legs, etc. The point is to engage in something requiring movement which will help act as a "vent" for the rising adrenaline levels coursing through the body in preparation for the fight and flight response.

Avoiding a meltdown in the first place

Avoiding it in the first place is the most effective way of preventing a meltdown. While this may seem like it needs no further explanation, it really needs to be clarified. A meltdown is often caused unintentionally, with only the best interests at heart, when the non autistic individual simply forgets for a moment that the autistic individual can't "take a break" from being autistic and places them in an environment that imposes too many cognitive or sensory challenges.

I cannot tolerate being at a crowded public venue where I am just a person amidst many others in the crowd because of accompanying sensory triggers magnified by a large crowd gathering. At a seemingly "fun" activity such as attending a sports event there are numerous sensory triggers that are often not taken into consideration when taking an autistic individual to such an event, especially if that non autistic person is "caught up in the moment" with anticipation (and sometimes frenzy) of the upcoming game. Whether it is a sporting event, parade, country fair, crowded movie theater, or concert, there will sensory triggers resulting from mass gatherings that can quickly become overwhelming and lead to a meltdown. Always be mindful of the hidden dangers of sensory overload by knowing if the autistic person you are with reacts negatively on a regular basis to certain triggers and then multiply that danger one hundredfold for this type of activity.

SENSORY TRIGGERS AT CROWDED GATHERINGS THAT ARE BEST AVOIDED BY NOT GOING THERE

- Crowded lines of people too close in proximity to one another.

- Difficulty distinguishing noises from voices.

- Fluorescent lighting or bright lights.

- Being accidentally pushed or shoved.

- Having to get up out of your seat once seated to let someone pass.

- Lengthy lines waiting to use the toilet.

- Overpowering smells of perfume, cologne, or refreshments being sold.

- Spontaneous jeers, applause, or yelling.

- Temperature change from many people being in a confined space.

- Competing with the noise volume in terms of modulating tone and volume when speaking (it becomes very draining to have to almost shout while speaking to the person next to you).

- The disruption of having a person next to you continually talking on a cell phone or in person to someone seated near to them.

Sometimes in an attempt to get autistic Timmy to socialize with his peers well meaning adults will enroll him in some after school sport such as soccer, basketball, American football, etc., encouraging both socialization skill building and team interaction. Particularly if the autistic child already has difficulty with socialization, the added burden of engaging in a recreational sport, which brings with it all the sensory issues I have just mentioned, may be too much to handle and could lead to a meltdown. The initial idea was to encourage interaction with peers but by focusing on that as the main goal they forget to take into account incidental sensory triggers that are magnified by the stress of having to socialize when not comfortable doing so. Sometimes meltdowns are a culmination of many triggers that keep adding up when exposed to a stressful environment without any chance of being able to remove themselves from that situation.

A final suggestion: learning to accept meltdowns as just part of who you are

I am leaving this as a suggestion because the following hint will have practical applications in only a narrow segment of the autistic population, but this technique is very effective in helping with maintaining our fragile self esteem. It is called "reframing." It is done in the post meltdown period when the autistic individual has had a chance to process what has happened and has overcome the embarrassment associated with that particular meltdown. It basically means revisiting the meltdown and changing (reframing) the negative image associated with it to a more positive one. By rethinking it in positive terms it helps us to "feel" like we aren't eternal failures, but just a fallible human like everyone else. Because there is so much pressure for us to conform to society's standards and norms, which are alien to us, the possibility of failure in those areas is a given. Adding uncontrollable meltdowns to our list of shortcomings only serves to batter our self worth. You can help greatly in this respect by not viewing the meltdown once it is over as something so serious that it should never be taken lightly. A meltdown is what it is, and to hold an autistic person emotionally hostage by reminding them continually of the gravity of each meltdown they had is detrimental to their mental well being.

Why do we laugh when we see someone else in an embarrassing situation that doesn't cause them physical harm, such as having their trousers suddenly fall to their ankles while walking across the street, or watching your co-worker taking a sip of coffee from their mug only to miss their mouth and dribble coffee all over their blouse? It isn't funny at the time to the person going through the embarrassment. We laugh because by doing so it is a way for us to forgive ourselves for some of the stupid or silly things we do. We laugh at others because we can identify with them and think to ourselves, "But for the grace of God, there go I."

Even the "victim," once they have had a chance to process what happened, will laugh at themselves. I find myself in these situations so often, mostly due to my autism, that I could feel suicidal if I didn't learn to laugh at myself and reframe it in such a way as to have others who hear my tales of woe empathize with me. I write a regular column about these misadventures, many which resulted in a meltdown, for the newsletter of the autism society chapter in my home state. You can access all the stories I write for them through my website: www.autistic-raccoonlady.com.

I am enclosing my latest article, which reframed an experience that almost lead to a meltdown at a public beach, as an example of what I am advocating. My lack of executive functioning skills seems to be the catalyst for these unfortunate scenarios. It wasn't the least bit funny at the time but now, months later, I can see the humor in the situation and I receive regular emails from readers who say they enjoy these stories so much. It also helps me talk about these near meltdown, meltdown, and poor executive functioning episodes in a way that is constructive and helpful with others who offer empathy and view my frequent meltdowns as just part of me and not a crippling limitation in my life.

This incident occurred while I attempted to wind sail for the first time at our nearby lake.

Getting the wind knocked out of my sail

A while back I bought a multi-sport inflatable watercraft on clearance at the sporting goods store. The photo on the package looked impressive, with a petite female model that reminded me of a Malibu Barbie doll waving to her friends on the beach while carrying this craft in its four-foot carrying case slung over her shoulder. I figured if a stick figure could bear the weight then it shouldn't be too heavy for a middle aged slightly overweight woman with joint problems like me. The package boasted photos of a tanned male model that reminded me of Barbie's boyfriend Ken enjoying its multi-use as a kayak, sailboat, wind sail, and tow behind raft for a speed boat. Based on the packaging, I couldn't resist. After all, how hard could windsailing be when Ken and Barbie made it seem so effortless?

Eager to get to the lake I took out the contents of the package for assembly. The first step was to use the foot pump to blow up the inflatable base. Once inflated it expanded into a six-foot long, four-foot wide blob. It was very cumbersome as I tried to wrestle it into the back of my pickup truck. Forgetting about the hard plastic keels I attached, I misjudged the clearance of the tailgate as I heaved the thing up causing the rubber nose to smack the tailgate and with the spring of a super ball bounce itself, with me still attached to the "easy carry handles," to the pavement four feet away.

Not easily deterred I then assembled the mast and sail which measured 12-foot tall and six-foot wide. The only way it would fit in the truck was by finagling it so the mast went through the rear window and hung out the passenger window by three feet.

The public boat landing where I went has a small beach beside it and that day there were about eight families swimming there. As I pulled up to the boat ramp in my pickup truck, which looked like it had been impaled by a gigantic blue and white striped nylon knitting needle, this unusual sight became the focus of their attention. It seems to be an unwritten social rule of the non autistic world that if you unload a watercraft of any sort at a public landing it is expected that you are a seasoned pro in that sport. I am sure my overconfidence in mastering this sport as I unloaded my gear was perceived as sign that I have done this a thousand times flawlessly.

All eyes were on me as I paddled out 100 feet on my new wind sail. The first clue that I didn't know what I was doing was that I forgot you need wind to wind surf and it was dead calm. Not wanting to look like an idiot I laid the mast down on the raft and practiced paddling techniques as if that was my intent all along. It was difficult trying to paddle a four-foot wide raft on my knees but I did it for an hour. Finally I felt confident enough to practice standing up so I could get a feel for the balance required for wind surfing. It was 0.003 seconds after attempting to stand that I realized my legs had turned into two bowls of pudding. It didn't occur to me at that moment that with two torn ligaments in my knees I lacked the stability and balance to maintain an upright position. I went crashing down as hard as the Hindenburg but unlike the zeppelin, which burst into flames, I bounced off the rubber and became airborne only to do the most ungraceful belly flop in history right into the water a few arms' lengths away from the raft.

My sunglasses flew off my face and instantly turned into a 10 pound rock, elusively thwarting every underwater swipe of my hands trying to grab them. Today they are probably still smugly perched on a submerged log 100 feet on the bottom of the lake. Spotting my sunhat bobbing in the water I looked like a golden retriever as I dog paddled over to fetch it and after placing it in my mouth dog paddled back to the raft.

Once I climbed on the raft I noticed my sail was completely submerged a few inches under the water. I tried lifting the sail up but it was if the Lady of the Lake had a death grip on it and it refused to budge. I was becoming really frustrated and angry at this point so I lay down on my belly, dangling my legs over the edge in hopes of gaining some lifting leverage. During this retrieval process I didn't realize in all my thrashing and limb flailing that my foot was up against and rubbing the one and only valve stem (the point to inflate or deflate the raft). After an epic struggle of woman verses the natural law of physics I felt this wave (no pun intended) of victory as the sail began to rise as simultaneously a stiff breeze kicked up. I couldn't help but notice the stream of bubbles emanating from the stern (rear) of the raft but in all the elation over my recent victory, all I could jokingly envision was that my craft had a bad case of flatulence.

Just as the mast and sail were half way righted, a sudden gust of wind from an approaching storm cloud grabbed the sail while I was still attached to it and propelled it forward and up so for a flash second I was actually standing up on the raft. Instantly I noticed that the raft had become spongy because it was in fact leaking air, not troubled with a bad case of flatulence, making it impossible to maintain the textbook perfect windsurfing pose demonstrated on the box by Malibu Ken.

It was now obvious that I was trapped on a sinking ship (again, no pun intended). Having no idea how to steer this deflating overrated air mattress, it began to act like a bunking bronco spinning in circles, and then lifting its front end followed by the back end. I was being whipped about like a rag doll. It pretty nearly convinced me that my multi-water sport craft was in fact possessed by a demon and my only salvation lay in an impromptu exorcism. I yelled out, "I rebuke you, demon of the multi-sport all purpose watercraft!" but it didn't help. Then without warning the wind shifted direction, ripping the mast out of its base, sending the mast and me flying. Out of principle I didn't let go because I harbored delusional thoughts that somehow I could still regain control, along with a shred of dignity, from this unfortunate series of events.

The wind gusts were in excess of 20 mph. I was hanging on for dear life to the boom (the rigid cross brace of the sail that controls the sail's direction) which was trailing behind the raft, when the watercraft demonstrated yet another talent not shown on the box… it became a speed boat and now I was water skiing. As this demon-possessed evil air mattress sped across the lake I was attempting to slow it down by throwing my weight backwards. That was as effective as trying to stop a moving vehicle by holding on to its bumper. By now the wind was so fierce and because I didn't have a script for this (remember it was dead calm when I first started), my only logical action plan was to hang on and master the art of wind sailing despite the odds. To add to my humiliation there was a growing crowd of people on shore pointing in my general direction. I quickly scanned the lake hoping they were looking at someone other than me but, alas, I was their freak show. I never prayed so hard for the Loch Ness monster to be real and magically have swum from Scotland to Maine just to devour me in that instant.

In all the commotion I didn't realize the water was getting shallow as the raft zoomed towards shore. The keel caught on a huge submerged rock, abruptly stopping this demonic beast. It literally knocked the wind out of the sail sending me tumbling like a tumbleweed onto the boat ramp and depositing the mast and sail in the tree grove along the edge of the shoreline. As I was gasping for air, a crowd gathered around me asking if I was alright. I was totally mortified by this spectacle so in a low voice I uttered, "I am O.K.; I just got the wind knocked out of my sail."

By creating either a mental or actual "re-write" of what happened into a more light hearted account it doesn't diminish the seriousness of what occurred. Instead it allows others to perceive the situation as just part of being human in an imperfect world as opposed to micro-analyzing what dysfunctional element of autism caused the debacle. Sometimes people tend to over analyze, because the person has autism, to pinpoint what autistic deficit was the source of the event. Not every mistake or mis-step I make is a direct result of my autistic limitations. Sometimes things just happen. Maybe the universe creates these opportunities as a teaching tool to remind us to "lighten up" and laugh a little.